Some thirty years ago  when we sat together at It became a most enric was as much social as m .... spent time on several occasions in Trinidad and other islands he oversaw and he visited our church and home time and again in Southern California. I remember how I could never get enough of hearing Peter humbly recall his miraculous boyhood and youth and share incidents of God's favor upon his apostolic ministry that began early in his life. I was so captivated by the Lord's workings that I would persistently nudge him to recount his experiences over and over. I have been blessed to have him as a friend as I saw him as a genuine and authentic man of God. Those of us who knew him best speak authoritatively of his genuineness and authenticity. Every remembrance I have of Peter brings me great joy. I am delighted that others will be able to catch a glimpse of this man through Doug Cowie's intimate account of Peter, his life, and his ministry.

—Dr. Paul Risser, Former President
International Church of the Foursquare Gospel

The work that Jesus began still continues. And that's what the book of Acts is all about—starting out from where Jesus left off. "The former account [which I prepared], O Theophilus, I made [a continuous report] dealing with all the things which Jesus began to do and to teach" (Acts 1:1, AMP). Reading *Acts 29: The Ministry of Peter Hosein* is like reading the Book of Acts. It whets my appetite (even as an older minister) for the supernatural. We can become so bogged down with the doctrinal that we miss the demonstration. And the true gospel is seeing the demonstration of God's power changing real-life situations. The followers of Jesus prayed (in the Book of Acts) for God's hand to be extended through them to see miracles happen. And they did. They were the norm. They were expected. And they were experienced. This book stirred my heart and I know it will for any follower of Jesus, no matter where they are on their journey with Him. It helps me "Watch for God" every day to join Him where He is working.

—KEN HISER, SENIOR PASTOR
FAITH MEMORIAL CHURCH, SANDUSKY, OH

This book gives a powerful example of how the Holy Spirit sovereignly enters the life of an unlikely young man, in this case a Muslim, and uses him to touch the world.

—DR. JIM BENNETT, DIRECTOR OF MINISTRIES
GLOBAL INITIATIVE: REACHING MUSLIM PEOPLES

Unfolding much like the biblical Acts of the Apostles, Douglas Cowie's book has captured the intriguing and adventurous life story of Caribbean evangelist and church planter, Rev. Peter Hosein. Told firsthand and through the eyes of those who knew him best, Hosein's life and ministry, spanning half a century, forged a legacy lived on through countless thousands who witnessed and received salvation, deliverance, healing, and provision. From his life-transforming vision of Jesus as a child to his home going in 2002, the tongue of this modern-day Paul was loosed to speak the Word of God, with supernatural signs and wonders following. The intention of the author is not to recount the life story of one rare exception, but to reveal the amazing potential that will come to any and every life fully surrendered and totally reliant on the leading and empowerment of the Spirit of the living God. Peter Hosein was just that sort of man—a true, contemporary apostle of the faith, whose preaching, humility, and dedication lives on as an inspiration to all who would follow in his footsteps.

—DR. TOM KEINATH
PASTOR, CALVARY TEMPLE, WAYNE, NJ
PRESBYTER, NORTHERN SECTION, NEW JERSEY DISTRICT
ASSEMBLIES OF GOD

When some Christians hear the words "apostle" or "apostolic," they are immediately on guard, even suspicious of such descriptions and labels. Some have cessation theologies that confine apostolic work to the first century after Christ. Others are willing to acknowledge the apostolic function but hesitate to declare an individual an apostle for fear of over elevation or misunderstanding. Other believers, especially Charismatic/Pentecostal adherents, use the term with abandon, assigning it to a variety of trans-local leaders with multifaceted ministries.

Peter Hosein's story is worthy of attention regardless of labels or traditions. God used this humble servant to bring the gospel to hostile communities and validated the preaching with signs and wonders. What makes this entire narrative so compelling is that Peter Hosein was not raised in a preacher's home and his life and mission had none of the "bells and whistles" that accompany so many self-proclaimed apostles.

Cowie does an excellent job of allowing Hosein's story to speak for itself. Down-to-earth people attest to the miracles, and the fruit of his ministry still exists in the many churches and ministries that flourish today.

This book engenders hope for all ministers evangelizing difficult and resistant populations. God's gifts are still available, and the supernatural remains our greatest witness. Apostolic ministry did not cease with the death of St. John— it is alive and well in humble women and men who pioneer kingdom endeavors!

I commend this work to all who need their faith lifted, ministry energized, and vision expanded.

—Dr. Charlie Self,
Professor of Church History
Assemblies of God Theological Seminary
Springfield, MO

Doug Cowie has intensified my desire to fulfill the Great Commission. Doug's book reinforces the fact that God is not a respecter of persons but will use any willing sacrificial vessel to spread His love. This is a great story demonstrating the grace of God.

—Zollie Smith, Executive Director
AG U.S. Missions, Springfield, MO

I have just finished Doug Cowie's manuscript *Acts 29: The Ministry of the Peter Hakim Hosein, Apostle to the Caribbean.* I found it to be most inspirational. It had a profound effect, much the same as spending Holy Spirit-led time in God's Word or in His divine presence in prayer. What an opportunity you have provided, to experience the power of God alongside a man as blessed as Peter Hosein! Your concluding chapters convicted me to recommit my life and household to righteousness. Being moved to seek after the anointing of the Holy Spirit, I now realize more completely the importance of prayer and fasting. I am grateful that God lead me to you and you to share this work with me. This biography is like rain in the desert. May God bless you and this manuscript!

—Sophia Peluso, Director
Sophia's Worshipful Ballet & Dance, Whitehouse, NJ

Acts 29:

The Ministry of
Peter Hakim Hosein
Apostle to the Caribbean

W. Douglas Cowie

CREATION
HOUSE

ACTS 29: THE MINISTRY OF PETER HAKIM HOSEIN, APOSTLE
TO THE CARIBBEAN by W. Douglas Cowie
Published by Creation House
A Charisma Media Company
600 Rinehart Road
Lake Mary, Florida 32746
www.charismamedia.com

Unless otherwise noted, all Scripture quotations are from
the Holy Bible, New International Version. Copyright © 1973,
1978, 1984, 2010, 2011, International Bible Society. Used by
permission.

Scripture quotations marked KJV are from the King James
Version of the Bible.

Scripture quotations marked NAS are from the New American
Standard Bible. Copyright © 1960, 1962, 1963, 1968, 1971,
1972, 1973, 1975, 1977 by the Lockman Foundation. Used by
permission. (www.Lockman.org)

Although the testimonies are real and verified, the names have
been changed.

Permissions obtained where possible.

Design Director: Justin Evans
Cover design by Terry Keenan

Visit the author's website: focus1.org.

Library of Congress CataloginginPublication Data: 2014941152
International Standard Book Number: 978-1-62136-760-4
E-book International Standard Book Number:
978-1-62136-763-5

First edition

15 16 17 18 19 — 987654321
Printed in the United States of America

CONTENTS

FOREWORD

A S A MISSIONARY serving in the islands of the West Indies I was eager to get my hands on this book by Pastor Doug Cowie who's been a friend of ours for many years and even helped prepare us before going to Curacao.

What I learned upon reading this biographical work is that it's not only about a particular servant of the Lord, but there are principles and dynamics reflected in these pages that transcend any specific place, person, or period. While reading this manuscript I felt as though I were reading accounts that could have been from the book of Acts. Well, let's say this book provides a glimpse of what God is doing in Acts 29, amen?

What stood out to me is not so much how great this man was but how great our God is, in empowering a vessel truly yielded to His service. Something that impressed me was the simple emphasis on the basics. Peter Hosein devoted himself to prayer and Bible reading—and let's not forget the fasting. It is evident from this book that here was a man who walked extraordinarily in the special graces of the Master—even when others around him were not—and saw abundant fruit because of this.

Peter Hosein ministered in the supernatural power God. Perhaps if we can begin to have more of an attitude of going against the tide of our culture, the way he did, and of committing ourselves to the Christian disciplines, and of being diligent and trusting and 'lost in God' the way he was—we too will see more of God's Hand evident in our lives and ministries.

Though Peter Hosein began walking with God over half a century ago, his testimony is vital and relevant not only for the apostolic grace he moved in, but also in how he broke out of a non-Christian family and community— bearing the persecution—and even turned around and led many of them to the Savior. In a sense you can say that Peter Hosein has provided an inspiring example of how Christians can find the fire for the Lord even in the midst of a hostile environment. There are so many today in many parts of the world who can find strength and encouragement, in this regard.

And so I do recommend this work to *any* Christian— especially those interested in ministry for the Lord. And I appreciate the way that Doug Cowie, himself a very Spirit-led man of God, has humbled himself to the point of appreciating and displaying so clearly and graphically the work of *another* man of God, for whose testimony and contribution he discerned merited such a focused examination, because he saw the potential for blessing the Body of Christ.

My thanks to Doug for bringing to light a story that really should be told, and for doing it so vividly and in such a way that we can all be edified by insights to be gained from a life well-lived for God.

—Tim Pike
Assemblies of God World Missions

PREFACE

THIS BOOK IS more than a biography. It highlights the message lived and preached through a man as the Spirit of God led him from village to village, island to island throughout the southern Caribbean. The Reverend Peter Hakim Hosein's life spanned the latter three quarters of the twentieth century, and his ministry resulted in the planting of over forty churches, which, for a number of years, were affiliated with and under the covering of The International Church of the Foursquare Gospel organization. (Peter originally founded the IPA (International Pentecostal Association) in Trinidad early in his ministry. IPA then became an affiliate of Foursquare in 1988 and remained so until 2006, about four years after Peter had gone to be with the Lord.)

The purpose of this book is twofold. First, I would like to encourage ministers and Christians in general to restudy the ministries of Jesus of Nazareth and His disciples and model their own outreach to their world in a like manner. Second, I would like to invite those with diverse spiritual points of view to thoughtfully read the accounts of the amazing events reported in this volume and honestly consider what impact this may have on their lives.

I believe the average Christian's worldview is dichotomous. By this I mean that we often view life as though it were divided into two compartments: secular and religious; and we act and think in a manner appropriate to the setting.

When we are at work or school, we participate according to the polity of that environment. At church we try to act in a manner spiritually compatible with our particular sect.

Perhaps we can learn from Peter's life and from those who knew him that there is a better way. Life can and should be lived 24/7 in continuous contact with the living God, and the results will be a life lived in the most efficient manner conceivable. Check out this work. Give it a chance to boost your output in life. You just might end up changed in a most exciting way.

Many books have been written as pure biographies; many written on evangelism and many to show Christians how to act and to relate to one another. This book is written as an adventure, but with normative information. It reports the highlights of the ministry of a man who obeyed his calling in life both in scope and manner. He thought, spoke, and acted in the supernatural, led by the Holy Spirit of God. Accordingly, he gave God all of the credit for whatever accomplishments he experienced, and there were a myriad.

INTRODUCTION

A NUMBER OF ILL-INFORMED, would-be historians have tried, of late, to bring into question the character and motives of fifteenth century explorer, Christopher Columbus, Nevertheless, the carefully documented records clearly show that he was not only a godly man but a man on a divinely-directed mission to spread the kingdom of God when he discovered what is now known as the Western Hemisphere. He truly believed that he was reaching his planned destination, the Indian continent, and that he would be an instrument of God to spread the truth of Jesus Christ to that part of the world.

Of his own faith, he is quoted thus:

> I am a most unworthy sinner, but I have cried out to the Lord for grace and mercy and they have covered me completely. I have found the sweetest consolation since I have made it my whole purpose to enjoy His marvelous presence. No one should fear to undertake any task in the Name of our Savior, if it is just, and if the intention is purely for His holy service.[1]

Of his mission,

> It was the Lord who put it in me to sail to the Indies. The fact that the gospel must be preached to so many lands—that is what convinced me. Charting the seas

is but a necessary requisite to the fulfillment of the Great Commission of our glorious Savior.[2]

That was AD 1492. During his third voyage to the Western Hemisphere, six years later, on Tuesday, July 31, 1498, he sighted Trinidad, and gave it its name (Spanish for "Place of the Trinity") after seeing three mountain peaks in the Grand Chemin area along the south coast. Although Columbus did not achieve his goal of reaching the people of East India with the gospel, God eventually had East Indians sent to Trinidad as indentured servants of the British colonials. On May 30, 1845, the *Fath Al Razak* carrying the first contingent of 225 Indians arrived; that date is celebrated much as the arrival of the *Mayflower* on 1620 is remembered in the U. S. This immigration of Indians as indentured workers would go on until 1915.

There in Trinidad they would not only learn of Christ's liberating message, they would join Columbus as fellow crusaders with him.

One such man was the Reverend Peter Hakim Hosein of the Princes Town area of southern Trinidad, only a few miles from where Columbus first looked on that lovely island.

Why would God be so intent on the spread of this message? (*Note: all italicized, inset passages are author's comments.)

The world is populated with an abundance of people who secretly long to be and do good, but know that their will-power will always disappoint them—people who hunger for authentic love, both given and received, but cannot even define the term—people who crave freedom, but have never experienced it. The following is an example from life.

...I wondered what real freedom would be like

In the early 1980s the author hired an architect, who had lived the first three decades of his life in the USSR, to come on staff with a large international consulting firm. He had been a card carrying member of the elite Communist Party and, as he put it, one of the privileged five percent that ruled and prospered in the Soviet Union. Nevertheless, he and his wife were left with a deep hunger that could not be satisfied, even with his successful attainment to high academic and bureaucratic status. He said to me, "All my life I wondered what real freedom would be like....I knew I had never experienced it." Because of his Jewish ancestry, he and his wife were able to take advantage of a brief window of opportunity to leave Russia—an opportunity not afforded other Soviet citizens who were forbidden to leave under penalty of prison or death. Within hours of departing Moscow by air, they arrived in Berlin on a layover. They decided to briefly step outside the terminal to observe a piece of that city. They were suddenly struck with the realization that for the first time in their lives no one was watching them or even cared who they were. This was their first taste of freedom!

The horror of what they *had* considered normal in their past life suddenly hit them. Their empathy toward the millions of "slaves" they had left behind began to generate a blend of anger and grief in their souls and hearts. At the time I interviewed the man, he had been away from his home country about two or three years. By then he had developed an insatiable hatred toward his old leaders. But there is a greater slavery.

We know...we are not playing by the rules

An even greater slavery exists in the world today; it is slavery to the fear of failing to survive and to be fulfilled in life. Mankind has been equipped with a genetic capacity to be able to sense the existence of a superior authority, a superior intelligence that overshadows and ultimately controls the destiny of the universe—God. The dominant element in the hierarchy of fear is the fear of ultimate retribution dealt out by this "God." May I say it another way: We know deep down inside ourselves that we are not playing by the rules. Someday we are going to forfeit the game—we are going to lose! And the penalty, whatever it is, will be horrible.

From the beginning of man's appearance on earth up until the present, people all over the world have tried to develop a fail proof solution to this problem to no avail. They have creatively invented philosophical and religious answers whose sole purposes are the relief of painful consciences. Speaking one morning with a psychologist, I was affirmed in my thinking that most human behavioral problems stem from unresolved guilt. In addition, there are those among us with such a misguided supernatural worldview that they have even attempted to influence what they perceive to be the governing spirit realm with occult methods and incantations. Their dark purpose is to obtain selfish advantage over others. Typical of this approach is Wicca, voodoo, Obeah, powwow, astrology (consulting horoscopes), palm reading, and the like. All of these practices have been specifically banned by God. His loving desire is for people to come to *Him* for help, not the other source—Satan. In Deuteronomy 18:9–13 we read:

> When you enter the land the LORD your God is giving
> you, do not learn to imitate the detestable ways of the

nations there. Let no one be found among you who sacrifices his son or daughter in the fire, who practices divination or sorcery, interprets omens, engages in witchcraft, or casts spells, or who is a medium or spiritist or consults the dead. Anyone who does these things is detestable to the LORD, and because of these detestable practices the LORD your God will drive out those nations before you. You must be blameless before the LORD your God.

True freedom and prosperity

True freedom and prosperity can only be achieved through the direct provision of God Himself and only through the approach that He alone has prescribed. I have a good friend who was living in the blessings of a carefully prescribed medication. Somehow a generic version was offered as an economical substitute by the health care industry, and he began to suffer from the defective product. Although he continued to take the medication (which could even have been a counterfeit) its efficacy—the ability to heal—was absent. He began to revert back to his old state of health. The same is true when man tries to alleviate his own defective spiritual condition by practicing cures inspired by the devil, which are wrapped in the guise of human philosophy, religion, or any number of old and new motivational gimmicks. God alone can minister this cure that He alone has prescribed. Unfortunately most people are afraid to approach Him directly because of a very real fear of judgment.

God came into the world as a little baby...to communicate with us without scaring us half to death

The Lake Erie shoreline in western Ohio is traversed by a number of migratory bird routes between Canada and the central United States. It is not unusual during the spring and fall to see hundreds of ducks, geese, and other water fowl resting on the water surface just off shore. One morning recently I observed a strange sight: a small flock of ducks was bobbing in the water about half a mile from where I stood and in the midst of the flock was what looked like a man's head. As I looked closer with my binoculars, I saw that the ducks were decoys and the man a hunter. He was in an odd little craft that held him just below the surface, perfectly dry, with only his head and shoulders above the level of the water. It was a little "ark." Using this ingenious technique, the man could approach the ducks in their own environment without spooking them. In the same way that modern duck hunters hide among the decoys to reach the ducks they are hunting, God came into the world as a little baby, apparently helpless and vulnerable, in order to communicate with us without scaring us half to death.

Following an exemplary thirty-three year lifespan on earth, during which He demonstrated His control over life and death—even the very universe itself. He voluntarily took our sentence of death and hell upon Himself with all its pain and horror just so we could be restored to a loving relationship with Him forever. In addition, we would receive as a bonus the supernatural power of His Holy Spirit to enable us to live a restored lifestyle in fellowship with Him and all those He has helped. This enduement of power was the fulfillment of Ezekiel 36:26–27:

> I will give you a new heart and put a new spirit in you;
> I will remove from you your heart of stone and give
> you a heart of flesh. And I will put my Spirit in you
> and move you to follow my decrees and be careful to
> keep my laws.

God has clearly informed us that the guilt which infects us through our rebellion against him can only be resolved, and our relationship with Him restored, through the advocacy of His Son Jesus Christ, who willingly sacrificed Himself on our behalf. He satisfied our debt by serving our sentence of eternal damnation for us! He literally took each of us into Himself (vicariously) and died on the cross. We actually died in Him. When He later rose from the dead, we—*still in Him*—also rose. He became the "firstborn" of a new breed of mankind that was also "born again" to a new Holy Spirit guided and empowered life. Having been cleansed by His blood, we are invited to fully partake of His Spirit, much as was demonstrated by Him when He was baptized in the Jordan by John the baptizer at the outset of His earthly ministry.

(If the reader finds the above a bit obscure, perhaps difficult to fathom, ask the Holy Spirit of God to explain. He will do so in His time and in a way that is perfect for you.)

...a healing balm, nourishment from heaven

This exciting message, known for two millennia as "the gospel" (an Anglo-Saxon term for "good news"), is God's solution to all the world's problems. It is a healing balm, nourishment from heaven, and it is embodied in Jesus Christ the Lord who has made Himself available to His "bride," the church.

Since the beginning of time God has looked into the hearts of men and women from one end of the earth to the other searching for those who would abandon their own agenda and do what is necessary to please the One who created them, even though they had never really met Him personally. In their spirit was a seed planted by God that thirsted for the warmth of His presence and the nourishment of His life. Such were Enoch, Abraham, Moses, Joseph, Ruth, Elijah, Isaiah, Ezekiel, and others. In southern Trinidad during the twentieth century, there were a handful of men called by God to carry the message of the gospel to the people of their region, people of varied cultures and religious backgrounds. God wanted His perfect and only prescription filled and the people of that area healed.

The Reverend Peter Hakim Hosein was such a man, and it is how God distinctly used him—not only to convey this message to his region but to build an army of workers to continue his work beyond the limits of his own capacity and lifespan that this biographical sketch is about. This epic reads a little like a modern day version of the Book of Acts, and the theological orthodoxy of Peter's actions and proclamations in his ministry have been validated throughout with reference to the Holy Scriptures.

Born to a Muslim family in a Muslim village on July 24, 1928, as the apparent answer to the prayers of a god-seeking father, Peter's ministry covered almost the entire latter half of the twentieth century. He went to live permanently with his beloved Master on March 16, 2002. The author found it interesting to learn from a family member that the month and the day of the month was the same as his baptism as a Christian and the same as his date of marriage twenty-seven years later.

Chapter 1
A CHANCE MEETING IN MIAMI AIRPORT

I T WAS A very frustrating Monday morning in June of 1993. Right about noon I checked in on my flight from Miami International Airport to Newark, New Jersey, on my trip home from Kingston, Jamaica. I had flown down about four days before on a Cornerstone Ministries International missions trip, hoping to meet with a well-known, high ranking Jamaican political figure. The expected interview was to be one of the steps in the fulfillment of our calling from the Lord to encourage the Jamaican church at large to begin focusing on the discipleship of men. My ministry partner at the time, Doug Norwood, and I had been shown by the Lord on a previous trip to the island that it would be through spiritually rejuvenated men that revival in the Caribbean would come.

I had received a phone call about two weeks before that one of the pastors in Kingston had arranged for the meeting, so I went down on the Thursday prior to await a specific appointment that was to be scheduled for sometime over the weekend. I sat in a hot muggy hotel for four days, not even able to use the pool for fear that I might miss the call and my trip be in vain.

Finally, on Sunday afternoon a call came, but not with the news I was waiting for. I was told that the official had an unexpected need to leave the island and that my visit would have to take place at some future date. I called the airline, made arrangements for a flight out the next morning, and arranged for an early morning check-in with the rental car I had been using.

Not at all happy with what happened, I considered the entire trip a waste. But, it doesn't end there. My partner and I believed that part of our ministry was simply to live and demonstrate the biblical concept of limiting all activities to those which have been clearly, personally specified by the Lord. This means staying in the center of His will at all times, avoiding sin so that His voice remains clear to us. My first thought was, "Where did I fall short?" (See John 5:19.)

At our previous board meeting, several of us had discussed what seemed to be a "leading by the Spirit" to start a work in Trinidad, even though we were not sure just where and with what approach. Our parachurch missions organization, Cornerstone Ministries International, came into being as the result of a vision given to my partner during a missions trip to Suriname. He was shown, quite graphically, that God was starting a revival in the Caribbean and that the "fire" of the Holy Ghost was going to sweep the entire ring of islands and coastal regions. Trinidad was in the "target" area. Had I not listened carefully enough? Had I gone off track? Perhaps, when I get home I had better pray for some door to open in Trinidad and get back on *His* agenda.

The "self-talk" began: "Oh, well. I'll make the most of what remains of the trip. I'll reserve a window seat in the middle of the plane with a good view, get a good magazine, enjoy the lunch, and forget about this disaster until I get home." This should not be the thought pattern of a Spirit-filled believer. Since I had about an hour layover, I would go over to one of the great Cuban juice bars in the main concourse and get one of their famous nonalcoholic piña coladas.

Instead, I spent the next half hour pleading with the attendant at the gate; there must be at least one window seat, especially since the plane was a giant Airbus and that the Monday morning flights back to Newark were usually "deadheads" with few, if any, passengers on the manifest. She agreed; but for some maddening reason, the computer simply refused to give me a window seat and, further, put me in an aisle seat next to another passenger so that it would even be impossible for me to slide over to the window at takeoff. By the time I had given up trying to show the attendant how she might correct the problem, my juice "window" had closed.

I was convinced that I had now entered God's punishment phase and wondered how long and how painful this was going to be.

I boarded the plane and walked down the starboard aisle to take my seat, appalled that the plane was, in fact, virtually empty. All of about five percent of the window seats were occupied, and that "dumb" computer would not give me permission to sit in any one of the remainder! So, I sat down next to someone who, out of the corner of my eye, appeared to be a mature businessman in a dark suit. Normally when I fly my first action is to pray that God would give me the opportunity to share the gospel with my seatmate, even to allow me to introduce him or her to Jesus Christ. This time, however, as I sat under my dark cloud of pity, all I could think about was how I might shuffle over to a window seat once the doors were closed just prior to "pushback." I didn't seek the Lord in any of this because I did not think that He was listening to me anymore anyway, and even if He was, I would not be able to hear Him.

As I sat there, trying to pass the time, I glanced over my right shoulder and noticed a small cross on the gentleman's left lapel. Hmm!

"Are you a Christian?"

"Yes, I am a minister with the Foursquare Gospel Church in Trinidad."

He was, in fact, the founder of International Pentecostal Assembly (Foursquare affiliate) headquartered in Trinidad and Tobago, with a number of churches and their pastors under his responsibility. When I outlined the mission to which God had called our parachurch ministry, he was quite interested and suggested that I contact him following his return from this current missions trip to Russia. He suggested that I prepare a presentation for his ministers as the first step to bringing Trinidad into God's program. Wow! The black cloud turned into a rainbow. What an awesome God!

I didn't know the half of what God had in mind.

As we chatted, awaiting the closing of the plane's doors, my new friend, the Reverend Peter Hosein, responded to my query regarding his initial entrance into the kingdom of God and his calling into the gospel ministry. My interest in a window seat had by now evaporated.

As I sat there waiting for the plane to begin to taxi out to the runway, Brother Hosein began to relate to me his personal testimony of God's direct intervention in his life— one of the most amazing I have ever heard. Somehow, as he began to talk, I knew that I must take notes; and I did. I filled two pages of a full-sized, college ruled composition book before he had finished. The date: June 8, 1993.

We exchanged addresses, phone numbers, and the like, and then spent the balance of the flight discussing our common perception of the state of the church universal.

And here was a doorway into one of our ministry's next areas of focus: Trinidad.

The following spring my partner scheduled a trip to Port of Spain, the capital of Trinidad and Tobago, as a result of an invitation by the Moravian Church there. We combined purposes, flew down together, and I met with Peter. I preached at his beautiful facility in Princes Town, Calvary Tabernacle (Foursquare), and met his lovely wife, Esther, and his son, Joshua, the assistant pastor. After the Sunday service I had dinner with the Hoseins at their home in nearby Moruga Road and spent a leisurely afternoon with them, discussing the general history of Peter's walk with the Lord and his work in pioneering approximately forty churches, most of which he was currently overseeing. I was particularly captivated by the stories of the supernatural power encounters that seemed to accompany almost all of his evangelistic and church planting work. It seemed as if his ministry was an extension of the Book of Acts—perhaps chapter 29.

I asked Mrs. Hosein whether anyone had taken on the task of recording these amazing accounts of God working through this very humble brother. She indicated that there was no such written record, but that there had been the acknowledgment of such a need. I suggested that I might consider helping with the task. A year later, in 1995, I began the work using a Marantz tape deck to do interviews. This book contains Peter's account of the Holy Spirit's work in his ministry, along with amplifications and commentaries inserted to authenticate the biblical concurrence with the anecdotes and theology reported.

Isn't God amazing in the intricate way He does things? I sometimes hear Him chuckling quietly about the way He is able to lead His workers in ways that not only surprise them but edify the entire body at the same time. What was initially planned as a trip to Jamaica, West Indies, for a pre-arranged meeting with the Honorable Michael Manley, that island nation's ex-prime minister, turned out to be a God-arranged meeting with the twentieth century's real person of influence in the Caribbean. Manley was seen by many, including Castro, as the man who could bring freedom to the West Indies. While his flame was slowly dying, God was raising up another man that history will show was perhaps the captain of a team that delivered the real source and means of freedom, not only to the entire Caribbean but to all who will read his story. That man was Peter Hakim Hosein. It is the Book of Acts continued.

In the four Gospels we read of the miraculous life and ministry of Jesus of Nazareth, the Son of God, as He demonstrated sinless life and authenticated His messages to mankind through signs and wonders that could only be performed through the creative power of Yahweh, the Father. As His earthly ministry was drawing to a close, He reminded His disciples of two critical points of instruction: (1) all that He said and did during His earthly ministry was precisely as He was guided, moment by moment by His Father in heaven (John 5:19–20); and (2) following His return to heaven, His disciples were to continue His proclamation of the good news of the reconciliation of God with mankind in precisely the same manner, using the same miraculous powers, not only to the Jews, but to the entire world (14:12–14). The actual start of this global ministry by His disciples was triggered by their empowering at the day of Pentecost, fifty days after Christ's ascension to heaven.

The New Testament book Acts of the Apostles, which immediately follows the four Gospels is the historical account that recorded the beginnings of the early church in

Jerusalem, featuring first the ministry of the apostle Peter and then focused on the missionary work of the apostle Paul, who was called and sent by God through the ministry of the Holy Spirit. The account of Paul's ministry was researched and recorded by a Gentile medical doctor by the name of Luke. The Bible records what many believe to be the Spirit arranged place of meeting between Paul and Luke to be Troas, the port of embarkation of Paul as he was led by the Holy Spirit to enter Europe with the gospel for the very first time.

Peter Hosein was heading to Russia when I met him in Miami. Can you see the interesting parallel?

But, now, let's allow Peter himself to begin his account.

Chapter 2
A YOUNG PRIEST IN TRAINING
Peter Begins His Personal Account

THIS BEGINS MY testimony of the marvelous things the Lord has done in my life. He has allowed me to serve Him for more than half a century, and His presence and power in my life seems as fresh today as the day I first met Him.

My grandparents came here to southern Trinidad from India as indentured slaves and settled in the little village of Cunjal, about four miles south of Princes Town. By the time I was born, there were about forty houses in that village; the population was entirely Muslim. The street was mud and the houses had thatched roofs. The only galvanized corrugated roof in the community was on our home. Being the most spacious building in the community, the Muslims used it as the mosque.

"If you give me another son, I will dedicate him to be the Imam."

The brother that preceded me died at the age of three. His death was taken by my father as a sign that he had, somehow, offended Allah. So he made this promise to Allah: "If you give me another son, I will dedicate him to be the Imam, the priest [of this village]." I was born soon after, the apparent reward for his consecration.

In those days, medical facilities were virtually nonexistent in our area; women relied solely on the midwives of the community. I was born early one morning on the dirt floor of my grandmother's home. Hearing me cry, my father came and asked, "What child is it that was born?" He was answered, "It's a boy." He responded, "Let us call his name Hakim. He will be the Imam." So, I was named Hakim. At the very tender age of four, my training began. My mother's brother, the Imam [or priest] started to teach me Arabic with the hope that I would eventually become his successor. Although I studied the Qur'an in English, I was taught that it could only be truly understood in its original language, Arabic, although many sects accept Urdu, the Pakistani translation.

At the age of eight I had fasted twenty-five days in the Muslim religion. During the month of Ramadan, the Muslim holy month, the ninth month of the Islamic lunar calendar, the Muslims fast from sunrise to sunset for thirty days. [*It is one of the five pillars of their religion.*] But I sensed, despite the fact I had helped my uncle or officiated as the under priest at the age of ten, that there was always an emptiness in my heart.

I had a longing, a searching...

I had a longing, a searching for something. I did not know what it was. As I look back, I can see the hand of God disturbing me, yet protecting me, as He drew me to Himself. We had no Christians in that community, and I had never seen a Bible in my life. I had never heard the name of Jesus. When it was time for me to begin to speak as a little child, my parents found that I was almost dumb; I could not speak. My frustration was driving me almost insane.

I suffered with a terrible speech impediment that caused me to withdraw from all contact with people. I never wanted to be in anyone's company. In fact, when I went to school, they made a public show of me. When the teacher would ask me to stand up and say something, the entire class would laugh; it was very embarrassing. I continued in this state; but got so frustrated that I started cursing people in the community without any justifiable reason.

Between the ages of nine and twelve I became overwhelmingly frustrated with life. My mother gave up on me. She said I would never make it. I was beyond her control. First of all, I did not realize at the time that the source of this frustration was spiritual in nature—a searching for satisfaction, the need to fill the emptiness in my heart. Secondly, it was magnified by the embarrassment I experienced over my speech. I became bitter against Allah for allowing me to be like that.

I narrowly escaped death many times

Besides having to withstand the inner battles I faced each day, the very neighborhood in which I lived posed its own natural challenges. I narrowly escaped death many times and only later realized it was by the hand of God. The community in which we lived was infested with a variety of poisonous snakes, including the highly venomous coral snake. One bit my twenty-one-year-old married sister, and in twelve hours she was dead. It was a terrible tragedy. I was ten at the time. One day I actually picked up a coral snake with my hand, not realizing what it was; another time [what appeared to be] a coral snake ran me down. I was fishing, and it came after the fish that I had caught. When I saw it, I started to run; it followed me home. There are two types of snakes: the small ones and the water coral, which is much larger. The small one, the type that bit my sister is also the more lethal.

I recall quite clearly another day I was fishing. My hook got stuck in a root. So, I went down into the water and tried to unhook it. I felt something slimy, and, thinking it to be a fish, held onto it and lifted it out of the water. Lo and behold it was a snake in my hand; I immediately shook it off. It was a water snake, and could well have been venomous.

Scorpions stung me about three different times, usually during the rice harvest. The rice is harvested from dry lagoons and placed on the bank. Then the rains come and flood the lagoons. This drives the scorpions from the lagoons into the rice on the banks. There are hundreds of them. They are really quite dangerous and can be lethal. If a scorpion stings you, you have to rush to the hospital as quickly as you can.

An irresistible desire came into my heart

Then, one day, at the age of twelve, I decided to stop by and pay a visit to my eldest (and married) brother at his store on my way home from school. (My father had given him a grocery store as his business.) I distinctly remember the irresistible desire that came into my heart that afternoon that I should stop by and just say to him, "Good afternoon." Although it would have been about one mile longer than the usual route home, I decided to stop and see him. However, ten or fifteen minutes before I arrived at his grocery store some rain fell and about five of us children took shelter under a tree.

While we were standing there, an eleven-year-old girl who was with us suddenly became frightened. She sensed that something, perhaps a ghost, had passed in front of her. So when we asked her what was the trouble, she said, "A cloud just passed in front of me, and I heard a voice saying from that cloud that you would be a great preacher." Well, I did not understand what it meant to be a preacher, or anything, so we just left it at that and I walked away. The group split up; each of us went our own way.

I went into my brother Tazmool's grocery store. As I walked in I saw a black book with a golden lining on a shelf and asked my brother, "What book is that?" He said, "It's a Bible. It tells about the Christian God and their religion." So I asked him if I could borrow it. He said, "Take it." I later found out that an African man from Grenada had become broke and came to my brother for sixty cents worth of groceries. All he had was his Bible, and so offered it to my brother in payment. My brother told him he didn't believe in the Bible—he didn't want the Bible; but the man left it with him. My brother shelved the Bible. When I "happened" to pass by that afternoon, I saw it and wanted to know about the Christian God. So, my brother gave it to me.

I put the Bible under my arm [and left.]. I did not realize that in a little while I would discover a continent [treasure chest] of miracles that would change my life forever. I had walked about a mile away from his store when I suddenly became anxious to know this Christian God. I flipped the pages of the Bible looking for a picture of the Christian God. Sadly there were no pictures of this Christian God, and so I said, "What a book!"

I came across the name Jesus...Jesus

But, eventually I saw a name that attracted me, the name John. And I knew that my uncle's name was Ramjohn, so I thought I would read something about this person John. I saw "New Testament, Old Testament," but I did not understand what it meant. It did not have any application to me. As I started to read the Gospel of John, I came across the name Jesus —Jesus Christ; and I was apprehended with His love, His mighty power and His miracles, and I was attracted to Him. So I started to read this Bible. Suddenly I found tears coming to my eyes.

> For the word of God is living and active. Sharper than any double-edged sword, it penetrates even to dividing soul and spirit, joints and marrow; it judges the thoughts and attitudes of the heart.
>
> —HEBREWS 4:12

> As the rain and the snow come down from heaven, and do not return to it without watering the earth and making it bud and flourish, so that it yields seed for the sower and bread for the eater, so is my word that goes out from my mouth: It will not return to me empty, but will accomplish what I desire and achieve the purpose for which I sent it.
>
> —ISAIAH 55:10–11

In the days that followed I would hurry from school, back home to read the Bible. I even began to share this new knowledge with my dear little friend, my cousin, and I started to tell him about this Jesus. How marvelous is this Jesus of the Bible! He's tremendous! And so, he would go home and tell his parents of this Jesus. Pretty soon the members of the community found out that I was talking about Jesus. My mother's brother came and told me that I was bringing a disgrace to the family and if I didn't stop they would disown me. I was warned that they would have to kill me or something, that I should stop, and that this Bible is not true. They said that the Bible was written by the white people to fool our parents from India and to cause them to become as slaves and such like. I heard all of this, but there was something that pulled me, drew me to the Bible and to Jesus!

One afternoon as I was sitting reading the Bible on our front steps an educated, seemingly religious man who belonged to the Anglican church came by and looked at what I was doing. He called out to my mother and asked, "What is this boy reading?"

"He said it's a Bible," she answered.

"Don't you know that people that read the Bible go crazy?" he responded.

So, my mother came down hurriedly and pulled the Bible away from me and said, "You heard what that man said. Don't you ever touch this book again in your life!" She took the Bible from me, and set it on a little shelf in the kitchen cupboard. I was so disappointed...so disappointed; I did not know exactly what to say or what to do.

But later, I went to the kitchen cupboard, took up the Bible, pushed it into a little brown paper sack, and I went out behind our house where a tree had fallen across a ravine. I sat in the grass, set the Bible on the tree trunk and I read...and I cried. After each reading session I would push the Bible back into the paper sack, put it under the tree trunk, and go home. Then, I would come back and read and cry for hours. One day my mother remarked: "You know, since you read that Bible, your life has changed. There is something that happened to you that has changed your life." I said, "My life is really changed; I love Jesus."

If you convince us, we will become Christians. But, if not...

One day, the community called a meeting of all the elders, a *Panchait*. I was about thirteen and a half by this time. They all gathered at a house in the village and asked me to come and explain about Jesus. In fact, my uncle came and said to me, "They are giving you a chance to tell us about Jesus; and if you convince us, we all will be Christians. But, if not, tonight is the last night you will ever mention this name *Jesus!*"

So, the Panchait was held. They invited two Muslim priests, one from Waterloo (quite a distance away from where we lived), and the other from Gasparillo. When they arrived, the elders of the community gathered and invited me into the meeting. Now, it was customary to sit on the floor, and I tried to sit down; but there was something in me that stirred me up. I did not realize at the time that it was the presence of God in my life. So, I said to them, "Listen, excuse me; I cannot sit, I will stand." And so I spoke, and I asked them this question: "Do you believe that the wages of sin is death?" They replied, "Yes." I then asked them to agree if there is no sin, there would be no death. They said, "Sure, death came as a result of sin."

"So," I asked, "why does a child die? That child has committed no sin. Why does a little child die?"

They said, "Well, your own Bible tells you that the sins of the parents will visit the children."

"Do you think that it is fair, that it is just, and that this little child should suffer— that an innocent child should suffer for the sins of the parents?" I said. "Well, that is the way Allah has it," they replied.

"Let me tell you," I said; "I believe that also, and this is a fundamental truth of the Bible. 'As by one man [Adam] sin entered into the world, and death by sin,' so by another man, [Jesus Christ] came the righteousness of God. 'For as in Adam all [of us] died, even so in Christ Jesus all shall be made alive.' 'For truly, the wages of sin is death. But the gift of God is eternal life through Jesus Christ our Lord.'"

Peter was quoting from portions of the following Bible passages.

Wherefore, as by one man sin entered into the world, and death by sin; and so death passed upon all men, for that all have sinned:
—Romans 5:12, KJV

But Christ has indeed been raised from the dead, the firstfruits of those who have fallen asleep. For since death came through a man, the resurrection of the dead comes also through a man, the resurrection of the dead comes through a man. For as in Adam all die, so in Christ all will be made alive.
—1 Corinthians 15:20–22

For the wages of sin is death, but the gift of God is eternal life in Christ Jesus our Lord.
—Romans 6:23

Within these scriptures are found the mystery of salvation. In essence, we are informed that the highly contagious disease of the sin nature was passed down to us as an inherited trait, through our genes—if you will, right from the time of Adam, our forefather. And, the only cure is one that is analogous to the cure of leukemia: in leukemia, the disease producing bone marrow is replaced by healthy marrow. Similarly, weak species of trees are strengthened through their being grafted onto disease resistant roots. In this case, when the seeker is grafted into Christ through spiritual rebirth, as was Peter Hosein, there is a miraculous healing of the soul and spirit. A transformation of the person begins to take place through the work of the Holy Spirit and the absorption of the written Word of God (the Bible). Often this is immediately accompanied by actual miracles of physical healing of the body.

My father's cousin was coming with a machete to kill me

Just as I was finished quoting these scriptures, I heard a scuffling outside the room where we met. My father's cousin was coming with a machete to kill me! The others held him down and took the blade from him...took away his cutlass! The owner of the house asked me to go home because he didn't want any murder to take place in his house. So I went through the back door and slept in the bush that night because I could not go home, otherwise they would bombard our house.

The following are quotes from the Qur'an:

But when the forbidden months /Are past, then fight and slay / The pagans wherever you find them. / And seize them, beleaguer them, / And lie in wait for them / In every stratagem (of war): / But if they repent / And establish regular prayers / And practice regular charity, / Then open the way for them: / For Allah is Oft-Forgiving, Most Merciful.

—SURAH 9:5, AL TAWBAH1

I should be declared...an outcast

That night they passed a resolution that I should be declared a *kujat*—an outcast. And I was not supposed to go into any home. They were not supposed to invite me to any dinner or any other social gathering; otherwise that house would be defiled. So I lived alone in the community. There were no Christians. I did not even know a song to sing. In fact, I did not even know how to pray. All I knew was to call upon Jesus...Jesus. But I was so happy, and I was so full of joy that I didn't even miss the company of people. I read the Bible and I called upon Jesus.

The persecution raged; there was more and more persecution. In fact, people scorned me in the community. They considered me a reproach; I was a *kujat*. And so, I had to live alone. But, as the persecution raged, I decided to fast, not from 6 a.m. to 6 p.m., but day and night. I read that Jesus had fasted forty days and forty nights, so I planned to fast and seek God. I did not know how to fast the Christian way, but I thought I should fast. So I fasted seven days and nights.

During the month of Ramadan, Muslims fast each day from sunrise to sundown; they compensate by eating what they want during the night hours.

It was like a funeral in the house

My mother thought I was going to die, and so, she started to weep, to cry, and to persuade me not to fast. My aunt came, and it was like a funeral in the house, what with the crying and wailing. So I decided that in order not to cause any kind of a great excitement in the place, I would break the fast. So I broke the fast after seven days and seven nights. It was a Thursday night.

Then I fell into a trance

I lay in my bed there at our home on Cunjal Road in Cunjal and began crying, asking, "Lord, why can't these people understand You? Why can't these people love and appreciate You? You are so wonderful. You are so glorious, so compassionate. How come these people don't understand You and can't accept You." I wasn't sleeping. I was just praying and weeping and asking God to give these people an understanding heart, that they might receive Him. Then I fell into a trance... fell into a trance!

26

In this trance I saw myself walking out in the bush with my Bible under my arm. I arrived at a junction and saw a Man standing there. As I lifted up my eyes and looked at Him, I saw His eyes penetrating me, looking straight through me. It seemed that He could see everything inside of me. I said to myself, "This Man is really marvelous. His eyes have such a force that they can penetrate me, and see inside of me." I kept walking toward Him. Then as I walked a few more steps, He called me by the name Peter. He said, "Peter." I looked up to Him; and He beckoned with His hands and said, "Come!" And so I went to Him. He spoke, "May I see your tongue? Let Me see your tongue!" So I opened my mouth and showed Him my tongue. He took a piece of stick about six inches long, about the thickness of my finger, and split it in two. He took one piece and bent it, and made a bow out of it. He then started to scrape my tongue. I noticed the spittle that came from my tongue; it fell to the ground like bundles of worms. He kept on scraping and scraping; I saw more worms fall from my mouth. I wondered and thought, "Lord, how come I lived with all this corruption in my mouth, and did not die?"

"A mighty storm is coming, and I am the shelter in the storm."

Suddenly, while He was scraping, what seemed like a fountain of crystal clear water burst open within me, and flushed out my mouth...flushed it out. He looked at me and said, "Now your mouth is clean. Go and preach the gospel."

I said, "I do not know how to preach. What shall I say to the people?"

He said, "Go, and tell the people that I am Jesus of Nazareth. A mighty storm is coming and I am the shelter in the storm." (See Isaiah 25:4.) So I came out of that vision, trembling like a leaf whistling in the wind, shaking... shaking!

When I got up that morning, I did not know, really, what had happened; and I went and told my mother in the kitchen. As I spoke to her, she stood up like a statue and looked at me. And then she asked, "What happened to you?" I said, "I don't know what happened." She said, "How are you speaking like this?" And I said, "Jesus of the Bible appeared to me last night and cleansed my tongue, loosed my tongue." She fell on my shoulder and started to cry. And then my little sister came and she started to cry. My little brother came and he started to cry also. And the three of them gave their lives to Jesus.

Some may wonder why Peter Hosein had to suffer with the affliction for so many years of his life. Was it because of the sins of his parents? Or perhaps his own? The Gospels speak well to this issue:

As he went along, he [Jesus Christ] saw a man blind from birth. His disciples asked him, "Rabbi, who sinned, this man or his parents, that he was born blind?" "Neither this man nor his parents sinned," said Jesus, "but this happened so that the work of God might be displayed in his life. As long as it is day, we must do the work of him who sent me. Night is coming, when no one can work. While I am in the world, I am the light of the world." Having said this, he spit on the ground, made some mud with the saliva, and put it on the man's eyes. "Go," he told him, "wash in the Pool of Siloam" (this word means "Sent"). So the man went and washed, and came home seeing. His neighbors, and those who had formerly seen him begging asked, "Isn't this the same man who used to sit and beg?"

—John 9:1–8

As the blind man was "sent" (Siloam, which is the Greek translation of the Hebrew Shiloh) by Jesus to witness to his neighbors, so Peter Hosein was sent to the communities in Trinidad by Jesus to tell of the wondrous works and the love of Jesus Christ. If the reader would like a good dose of righteous humor and a good preparation for understanding God's direction in Peter Hosein's ministry, I suggest reading the balance of John, chapter 9, right on through verse 41.

We had three rum shops, and that year the three rum shops closed down

That was the beginning. My tongue was loosed. From that day on I have never stammered or stuttered again. I was loosed. My family could not deny the miracle. And so, many of them came and asked what had happened. Then I had the opportunity to tell them how Jesus had loosed my tongue.

We had three rum shops, and that year the three rum shops closed down. My brothers and their families surrendered their lives to Jesus Christ.

Another noticeable thing happened once I began reading the Bible: the head teacher said, "I wish I could be like you." My life was truly changed and transformed. When I got that Bible, it seems to me I lost my desire for everything else but to read it. (The man who brought the Bible to my brother's store was originally from Grenada and lived in a nearby shack he had built. I really don't know if he got saved, but I have held onto that Bible until this day.)

Now I wanted to get baptized in water. I saw that I needed

to get baptized in water because Jesus was baptized and told the disciples that those that believed should be baptized. But the trouble was where to find a man to baptize me. I waited five years before a preacher came and baptized me in water; I was immersed on the twenty-fourth of July 1949.

Peter's study of the Holy Scriptures convinced him that baptism in water was Christ's will for him. Psalm 25 tells us that God will confide in the righteous. Further, we learn from the Epistle of James that God will give direction to those who ask (James1:5).

I heard myself speaking in a strange language

One night when my brothers and my cousins and I were playing cards—not gambling, just playing cards—I heard a voice inside of me saying, "Why don't you get up and go and read the Bible?" I did not recognize it was the voice of the Lord, so I continued to play. Then the voice came to me again and said, "Get up and go and read the Bible." [See 1 Samuel 3:4–10 for similar account.] So I said to them, "Listen to me, I don't think I want to play cards anymore; let me go and read the Bible." They said, "No, finish the game." I tried to finish it but my mind became a blank. I could not play.

So I set the cards on the table, got up, went and pulled out an old fashioned lamp that had been my father's, and started to read the 11th chapter of the Gospel of John. I came to the place where Jesus lifted up His eyes and said, "Father, I thank thee that thou hast heard me. And I knew that thou hearest me always: but because of the people which stand by I said it, that they may believe that thou hast sent me." Then Jesus "cried with a loud voice, 'Lazarus come forth'" (John 11:41–43, KJV). I suddenly found myself standing. I had been sitting and reading but when I came to that scripture, I stood up and started to shake. The Bible fell out of my hands; I fell on the floor and a mighty surge came over me, a power just surging through me, and I heard myself speaking in a strange language. The words just billowed out of the very depth of me. And I thought that if the Lord did not hold [back] this power I would die. The power of God just continued to surge through me.

When these boys and my mother heard me speaking like this, they ran out. They thought that what the Anglican man had said had come to pass—that I was, in fact, going crazy. But I could not help it; I was just lying there under the power of God. Then, after about an hour, I got up and went to bed. I did not speak to anyone. I did not know what happened, but that experience just changed my life—profoundly changed it!

Reference is made here to John 7:37–39:

Jesus stood and said in a loud voice, "...Whoever believes in me, as the Scripture has said, streams of living water will flow from within him." By this he meant the Spirit, whom those who believed in him were later to receive. Up to that time the Spirit had not been given, since Jesus had not yet been glorified.

The fulfillment of this promise by Jesus Christ took place for the first time during the Jewish feast of Pentecost, which immediately followed Christ's death and resurrection. At that time the disciples of Jesus were filled for the first time with His Spirit as the enabling power for holiness and ministry. (It is suggested that the reader study Acts, chapters 2 and 3.) This event was also prophesied in the Old Testament by Ezekiel 36:27 and Joel 2:28. The initial physical evidence experienced by the disciples was

> *a manifestation of the Spirit's presence in them involving*
> *their speaking in unknown tongues, and prophesying in*
> *their own language.*

I was preaching with might

Not long after that I stood out on the roadside and started to preach. People came—about 200. They wanted to see this little fellow preaching. I was preaching with might. When I reached about halfway through what I wanted to say, half the crowd fell down on the road—*half of the people actually fell down on the road*! I said, "Lord!" I did not know what happened.

> *Once a person has been baptized in the Holy Spirit, as*
> *Peter had that night while his friends were trying to keep*
> *him interested in playing cards, he (or she) has become*
> *a fully surrendered vessel of the Lord, (the Spirit) and*
> *amazing things can happen. Note the similarity of the*
> *above phenomenon to what those who arrested Jesus in*
> *the Garden of Gethsemane experienced:*

> So Judas came to the garden, guiding a detachment of soldiers and some officials from the chief priests and Pharisees. They were carrying torches, lanterns and weapons. Jesus, knowing all that was going to happen to him, went out and asked them, "Who is it you want?" "Jesus of Nazareth," they replied. "I am he," Jesus said. (And Judas the traitor was standing there with them.) When Jesus said, "I am he," they drew back and *fell to the ground.*
>
> —JOHN 18:3–6, EMPHASIS ADDED

> *We often do not realize that when someone comes*
> *into the presence of a Spirit-filled believer, that person*
> *has, in fact, encountered God. Too often, Spirit-filled*

believers try to hide this light under a bushel basket (see Matthew 5:15) out of fear of embarrassment or persecution, and those to whom God has sent them have missed out on a blessed encounter.

All I knew was that people wanted to follow Jesus

The traffic stopped. Those that stood up first had to drag the rest of the people out of the road. I asked, "Lord, if all these people die what would happen tonight?" And you know, from there on many people got saved. (At that time I did not know what it meant to "get saved." I did not understand the theology of salvation.) All I knew was that people wanted to follow Jesus. They came and they wanted to follow Jesus, and so we built the first church in Cumuto. And miracles started to happen. There were signs and wonders; just as Jesus said:

> And these signs will accompany those who believe: In my name they will drive out demons; they will speak in new tongues; they will pick up snakes with their hands; and when they drink deadly poison, it will not hurt them at all; they will place their hands on sick people, and they will get well.
>
> —MARK 16:17–18

The community where I lived was wicked; the people were wicked. There was a fight every day of the week. They would gamble and kill; there were about four murders in that area. But you know, by the time I had been walking with Jesus for about ten years, the entire village had come under the siege of the power and presence of God. We built a church in the town (about 1950).

Although they were initially amazed by the healing of my tongue, the Muslims continued to persecute me until

I left the community—about nine years later. Nevertheless, about 100 people in that town became saved [born again—see John 3:3] during that time.

I went to school until I was about fourteen years of age. Then I left school and went into business. We sold the property my father had left and established two other grocery businesses with the money. I controlled one in Cunjal and my other brother one a little further north. My family was quite well established in the business community. My grandfather had been a successful businessman. He planted sugar cane and sold it to the local factory from his twenty-two acres. By the time he died, my father had accumulated about sixty-six acres from which he grew rice and sugar cane and raised animals. He also ran a grocery store. I seemed to be heading into the same line of work. But the Lord saw differently.

My mother thought that I was going to die

When I was about eighteen years of age, I almost died. They thought it was TB, but it was not. I could hardly stand up. One night when my mother came to my room she asked, "Are you feeling pain?" I said, "Yes." I could not move my legs. It was as though I had died from my waist down. My mother thought that I was going to die by morning. I remembered reading what King Hezekiah did when he first faced death: he turned his face toward the wall (2 Kings 20:2). I did that, and I prayed. I said, "Lord, if You will raise me up, the rest of my life will be Yours." I was about eighteen at the time. The next morning, a Christian brother came to visit me with a book: *Atomic Power with God through Fasting*, by Franklin Hall. I read it and fasted, and in three days I was raised up. (Over the years my mother witnessed, first hand, the power of God

34

many times. Toward the end of her life, as she lay sick, some Muslim friends came to visit her. They told her to say Allah. She said, "No, it's not Allah; it's Jesus.")

I left my business. I gave it up. I walked out and started to preach. And in most places I went to preach, people got saved. We followed up by building a church in that location. We were reaching Hindus and Muslims.

Between the time he began his ministry at the age of twenty and the present, Peter established about forty Pentecostal churches: twenty-seven in Trinidad, one in Tobago, four in St. Vincent, three in Grenada, one in St. Lucia, one in Dominica, and two in Barbados. Except for the last four that went over to the Assemblies of God —they could not be adequately supported—and two of the Trinidad churches that went over to the New Testament Church of God, all were IPA/Foursquare churches, which he oversaw till his death. None are closed. Membership in all of these churches is reported to be growing.

Ye have not chosen me, but I have chosen you, and ordained you, that ye should go and bring forth fruit, and that your fruit should remain: that whatsoever ye shall ask of the Father in my name, he may give it you.
—John 15:16, KJV

Chapter 3
PETER'S FIRST MISSIONARY JOURNEY
Peter's Personal Account Continues

The primary emphasis of my ministry...the supernatural

The primary emphasis of my ministry was the supernatural power of God to deliver the people. I realized I could not reach them with mere words. God had to come and touch the people, do some healing and deliverance. In those days I fasted a lot; I spent a lot of time in fasting and praying. I wanted nothing to do with the world. I would read twenty chapters a day of the Word of God, the Bible —ten chapters in the morning before I had anything to eat and ten after I ate. Then, whatever Christian book I would put my hand on, I would read. The fruit came from this.

Many Christian leaders have come out of the ministry of Peter Hosein. Some have gone independent and have their own churches. Some are ministering in the United States and Canada. One well-known man of God, Dr. Stephen Mohammed, a seminary professor with the New Testament Church of God in Trinidad, came to Christ as a result of his family's conversion through a mission outreach of Peter Hosein. Peter was ministering in the supernatural at the Iere Presbyterian Home in Iere Village, Trinidad, where he had been invited to preach. There was a demon-possessed girl at the home. Peter prayed for her and

God delivered her. Stephen's father, mother, brothers, and sisters all got saved. Peter founded a church there after a week of revival services and became its first pastor. That church eventually became an affiliate of the New Testament Church of God. Dr. Mohammed's testimony is told in more detail in part 4 of chapter 10.

As Peter's ministry began to expand, there was the accompanying evidence of God's power followed by the enemy's attempted resistance.

"I have the asthma; I can hardly breathe."

A woman with an acute case of asthma was going to the spring to get a bucket of water. I was standing in front of our church in Cumuto and heard her wheezing. I said, "Sister, what has happened to you?" She said, "I have the asthma; I can hardly breathe." I said, "Come," and she came to where I was standing. I laid my hands on her, and said, "Lord Jesus, heal this woman." And instantly she was healed; the asthma went. She was a Muslim woman, yet she decided to follow Christ. She said, "I want to follow Jesus. Look what Jesus did for me."

The day of her baptism almost became the day of her death as well as mine! Her husband later admitted that he planned to kill both of us. In fact, earlier than my planned arrival in town that day, he hid with a gun along my route of travel, waiting to shoot me as I passed by. He had decided that I was to die. However, the night before the baptism took place, I had a dream that I was traveling on that very travel route and that an angel flew over me and came down and covered me. Now, I did not know that this man would be hiding with a gun to shoot me, so the dream seemed to have no meaning. The next day I headed for the church on my bike. As I reached a point about 300 yards short of where he was laying in wait for me, a man driving by with a truck suddenly stopped alongside me; he picked up my bicycle and put it in the truck. Then he opened the door, and said, "Come and sit down." I did. He then drove me to the church which was about half a mile further down the road. (Man…or angel?)

The woman's husband waited for me until 1:00 in the morning. He knew that I was going to pass that way with my bicycle and that was the night I was going to die. I later learned that the man concluded that perhaps something had happened to me, that I did not show up that night. But in the morning he saw me in the village and wondered how in the world I had passed by him. How did I get into the village?

The following week we held a revival meeting in the church, and I was preaching. He came with a stick to beat his wife. The wife decided to die for Christ. He stood up in front of the church with the stick, but after a while he left. That night he hit his wife with a bamboo stick and split her face. The woman had to run away from the house and seek refuge at a neighbor's. When they told me about it, I went to see her. I saw her face split in two and covered with blood. I asked her if she wanted to go to the doctor. She said, "No, I just want you to pray for me." I prayed for her, and the woman, Sister P, is alive today. You cannot see a trace of the cut.

The next night the man came back to his usual spot across the street from the church to wait for his wife. The presence of God was so real that when a boy made a little noise in front of him, he said, "Listen, if you don't want to hear what the preacher has to say you better go home." The third night he came again. This time he walked across the street, into the church, and gave his life to Jesus. I had the opportunity to baptize him also. It was after this that he told me of his attempt to kill his wife and me! He walked with Christ till the day he died; I praise the Lord.

...we are going to burn down this house tonight

One day, after her husband's death, Sister P left her mother's home and came to church. Some of her brothers were very upset with her because they felt that she was bringing a reproach to the family. So they came to their mother, and said, "Listen. You come over to our home and stay there, because we are going to burn down this house tonight; then Sister P will have no place to stay." But the mother said, "Why would you want to burn down the house. This girl is not doing anything wrong. She is just worshipping God according to her own conviction, and we should not be so cruel to her." So the mother persuaded these brothers not to do anything to the house. Nevertheless, when Sister P returned home, they came to beat her and to cast her out of the house. She fled to the home of one of her other brothers, who lived nearby. And this brother, although he was not a Christian, accepted her and told the other brothers, "This is my house, and you cannot interfere with my sister here. I want her here." So the brother sheltered her from that night onward, and she lived in peace. Wonderfully, one of her brothers is now saved and is a preacher. Sister P has since inherited her mother's home and lives there to this day. She has been an intercessor for the assembly ever since.

I visited Sister P on my second interview trip to Peter's home and found her to be a gracious saint and a true prayer warrior. Her joyful proclamation, "God is real," summarizes her brief talk with me. She casually mentioned the time when she had a headache; Peter happened to pass by and his shadow fell on her. Her headache was gone. Before becoming a

Christian she had attended the mosque, but "did not know what it was all about. I could not contact God." One day (about thirty-five years prior to our meeting and during the time when she was about five months pregnant with her sixth child), Sister P went out to milk their cow. After milking the cow she chained it a distance away. Suddenly the cow bawled and then ran; the chain, acting like a sling shot, flipped Sister P about ten feet. When she got up, her eyes began to go dark, and she felt a terrible pain in her back. She managed to get to the church service that night, seeking to be prayed for by Peter. During the worship and praise service she was healed. (The daughter she was carrying at the time sat there as we talked!)

...my sister-in-law began suffering with boils on her arm

Soon after my preaching ministry began, my brother accepted Jesus Christ as his Lord and Savior and found himself in serious conflict with his wife, who was raised in a devoutly Muslim family. As my brother and I began to meet in fellowship, my sister-in-law responded by simply ignoring us. One night, though, she actually closed the door to keep us out of their home.

In time, however, my brother succeeded in persuading his wife to allow us to begin a small worship service at the back of their home. During that initial service she came to me and asked for prayers of healing for one of their sons. Infected tonsils had caused a serious swelling of the face and a burning fever. I laid my hands on him in accordance with James, chapter 5, and within minutes he was instantly healed of all symptoms. The infection was gone.

Is any one of you in trouble? He should pray. Is anyone happy? Let him sing songs of praise. Is any one of you sick? He should call the elders of the church to pray over him and anoint him with oil in the name of the Lord. And the prayer offered in faith will make the sick person well; the Lord will raise him up. If he has sinned, he will be forgiven. Therefore confess your sins to each other and pray for each other so that you may be healed. The prayer of a righteous man is powerful and effective.

—JAMES 5:13–16

A few weeks after that, my sister-in-law began suffering with boils on her arm. This time she came into the meeting on her own behalf. I laid my hands on her shoulder, prayed, and rebuked the affliction. She left the meeting to go and examine herself; lo and behold the boils had disappeared.

A careful study of the four Gospels—Matthew, Mark, Luke, and John—in the New Testament will result in the clear realization that Jesus, during His three year ministry on earth, healed most of the sick people He encountered through a word of authority. He actually spoke to the affliction and commanded it to go out of existence. This approach is clearly in line with God's proclamation to the first man, Adam, where He gave mankind authority over every living thing. Since most sickness is biological in nature, it is not much of a stretch to understand the logic and the legitimacy of this means of healing. Sometimes there was evidence of some sort of prayer to His Father. Other times the mechanism seemed to be simply a laying on of His hands, such that the power of His divine vitality would flow into the recipient and healing would take place.

She gave her heart to Him

This miracle convinced her that Jesus Christ is the Son of the living God, and that He is mighty to save and strong to deliver. She gave her heart to Him.

This last action, of course, created a big stir in her family, and she was actually rejected. Her father told her, "You will not inherit any of my property, and when I die you are not to come and attend my funeral." To this she replied, "I don't think I need any property, for the Lord is my riches."

> For you know the grace of our Lord Jesus Christ, that though he was rich, yet for your sakes he became poor, so that you through his poverty might become rich.
>
> —2 CORINTHIANS 8:9

One day during the construction of the Cumuto church building, her youngest son jumped from the window ledge onto a piece of board with a protruding nail. The nail pierced right through his foot. We actually had to stand on the board while we pulled his foot off the nail. The blood spewed out. I laid my hands on his foot and prayed, and in less than five minutes the boy was walking normally. There was no trace of the injury. My sister-in-law is a faithful Christian and an ardent worshipper of the Lord Jesus Christ.

...born with a serious defect

My brother's daughter was born with a serious physical defect. When her mother gave her a bottle, the milk would run out through her nose and ears; no one could understand what was happening. Eventually they took her to the doctor. Upon examination it was found that there was no palate in her mouth. The doctor simply concluded that the child was born with a birth defect and that there was nothing anyone could do. The baby's mother returned home weeping. I was in my brother's store when she arrived. She described what the doctor had found and, quoting him, explained that there was nothing medical science could do about this. The child was simply born without a palate. My brother turned to me and asked, "Don't you think God can heal this child?" I said, "Of course! If we believe, there is nothing impossible with God" (Luke 1:37, KJV). So they brought the child to me. I laid hands on her and prayed in the name of the Lord Jesus Christ. Then I said to my sister-in-law, "Go and give her a bottle of milk." The baby took the milk; she did not vomit nor did it come out through her nose or ears. It stayed down. My brother was so amazed that he opened the child's mouth and looked inside. God had just done a creative miracle: the little girl now had a palate where before there had been none. That girl who is now in her mid forties regularly worships God at Queensway Cathedral in Toronto, Ontario, Canada.

During the mid 1970s the author participated in a small clergy support group that met once a week for a bag lunch get-together in Central New Jersey. At one point we were praying for God to reveal Himself to us in some dramatic manner. One day our Episcopal brother came in all excited. A couple who had only attended his church occasionally came to him asking that he baptize their newborn infant who was diagnosed with a terminal blood disease. He agreed to perform the ordinance, but during the ceremony asked to be allowed to anoint the child for healing. The couple, with a shrug, agreed. A week later they came rushing into the church office to announce that their child was now well. Canon P. smiled knowingly at them, telling them that he had expected as much. They went on, however, to tell him that the miracle was even greater than they had all hoped for. The child had been born with no palate. Now there was one, and God had made the baby perfect.

...dumb and crippled for no apparent reason

Another of my brother's daughters awoke one morning and found that she was both dumb and crippled for no apparent reason—she was twelve or thirteen at the time. Her mother had died, so my other sister-in-law took her to her home to care for her. One Wednesday evening I stopped by there and picked them up and took them to a prayer meeting at the Clarke Rochard church where there was regular prayer and fasting. On the first Wednesday we carried her in and prayed for her; seemingly nothing happened. We put her back in the car and took her back home. The second Wednesday, the same thing happened—no change. Again we brought her back home, still crippled and dumb.

My brother went to many medical specialists all over Trinidad. Whenever he heard of a doctor who might be able to help, he took his daughter there. There appeared to be no earthly hope. On the third Wednesday we carried the girl into the church and sat her down on the front bench. The group began to pray earnestly; I was up on the platform and joined them in prayer. After about a half an hour the girl cried out! She pointed over my head, and she said, "Look, an angel." Immediately, even as she spoke, her body was loosed. She was able to stand up. Her speech returned, and she was completely normal. She is married, has children, and has faithfully worshipped the Lord ever since.

Later in this book we have included a chapter in which Peter's son, Joshua reflects on his father's ministry from the family's point of view. The following account had originally been included in that chapter, but because of its foundational merit it has been incorporated here.

COMMENT BY JOSHUA HOSEIN, PETER'S SON

...my father would literally walk the soles off of his shoes

In the very early days of his evangelistic ministry, my father would literally walk the soles off his shoes as he went from village to village to preach the gospel. I remember him putting cardboard in his shoes when he had to go and preach. But while the soles of his shoes were being worn off, his own soul was becoming more durable, more solidified in the God who will not let him down. The Lord took him from walking the country lanes, to riding, to driving, to flights as far as Russia, even as far as the Holy Land. God has taken him from humble beginnings and has blessed his life.

After his feet began to bother him, the Lord provided him with a bicycle. Dad would put his Bible and books in a briefcase, strap them to the luggage rack of his bike, and ride to the various villages where he was called to preach the gospel. One night he rode up to the front of a store in Iere Village, leaned his bike against the wall, and started his message. As he began, he seemed to discern that two Hindu men had come up with the sole intent of robbing him. He kept "one eye on the Holy Spirit" and the other on his briefcase. After his sermon he went up to these two men and told them what he had seen in their hearts and that heavenly riches far surpassed those of earth. They cried; the Holy Spirit melted their hearts, and they were convicted of their sins. They repented and were immediately born again. Revival broke out there. The church that was started is now under the covering of the New Testament Church of God.

My father's ministry began to expand to many distant towns and villages. It suddenly became apparent that he should arrange a prayer conference with the Lord. The primary issue was the need for an automobile. He prayed, "Lord, if I am preaching this gospel, You are supposed to be taking care of my natural needs. And, Lord, I would be thankful if You would give me a little car." Then he described exactly what he wanted: a tiny little four-passenger English car called a Prefect. It was about four feet wide and maybe eight or so feet in length.

He told me that the reason he chose such a small car was because he felt that God had other needs to fulfill, and he did not want to exhaust God's supplies. Certainly God had to provide cars for other preachers too, did He not? Immaturity? Or humility? No matter! If God would supply the Prefect, dad would be happy and content.

So he continued to pray: "Lord, send me a car." One of his brothers said, "If you really have faith that this God you are praying to will send you a car, why don't you start right now to build a garage to keep the car in?" My father thought that that was a brilliant idea. So, although no car was in sight, he built a garage trusting in God's provision. One afternoon as he preached in San Fernando, a city in the southwestern corner of Trinidad, he sensed a mighty anointing of the Holy Spirit. The anointing carried over into the evening service as he presented the clear message of the gospel. Many people came to know the Lord through that service.

There was a man in the crowd who was, at that time, a millionaire. That night God dealt with him. The next day he inquired, "Who was that preacher last night?" The information was provided to him, and he proceeded to drive down to Cumuto where my father was living at the time. In those days the trip from San Fernando to Cumuto was a long, lonely drive over muddy back roads and lanes. Nevertheless, he found my father and asked him, "Do you have your car license, because the Lord has put it within my heart to give you a car." It was a Prefect, the same car he had prayed for! God had indeed provided for his servant. My father went and picked up the car, got his license to drive, and began using the car for the ministry. What a wonderful miracle! His faith had surely paid off.

PETER CONTINUES

The power of God just came down

One day I was driving along with a brother from Grenada. He noticed two little girls, sisters, standing at the edge of the road and suggested that we might give them a ride and drop them at their home. I didn't know them, but said, "Sure, I'll drop them off." So we dropped them off in the town of Gasparillo. As I let them out of the car, the Spirit of the Lord spoke: "Why not preach here?" So I asked the girls, "Would you all ask your parents if I could come and use the downstairs of the house to have some meetings?"

Their answer was, "If you come, we'll invite the people." So, we said, "Okay." We sent some boards and some concrete blocks for seats, and we started a revival. The power of God just came down in that place. I had no money, but the Lord said to me, "I want you to build a church here; you are to set up an altar where the people will come and praise Me."

The Lord gave me a sign that night: I dreamt we were in the meeting the following evening and the meeting was kind of dry; nothing seemed to be happening. I began to drag out the service, to cause it to linger. Then my wife [in the dream] said, "Why don't you close this service?" I responded with, "Well, you come and close it." Then a man stood up and said to me, "Don't be discouraged, God wants you to build a church here." That was the dream.

The next night I went back to the revival meeting. The service dragged along, exactly as in my dream! (I never told anyone my dream, not even my wife.) Then my wife said, "Why don't you close this service? I said, "Well, you come and close it," and immediately I recalled the dream! I had my confirmation. I stood up and told the people, "I want you all to look for a piece of land; God wants us to build a church here."

To better understand this sort of transaction with God, please read 1 Samuel 14:6–13, where Jonathan told his armor bearer that God would give them a sign which would let them know whether to make an attack or not. He said that if the Philistine soldiers in the fortification above them responded with, "Come up here," when he taunted them, it would mean God was affirming Joshua's victory.

...God told me that He'd give you this piece of land

Two days later I was driving along the road going to the revival meeting with a brother, who was an associate in our ministry, and I stopped to visit one of the families attending the meetings. While I was in their house speaking to them, this brother got out of my car and walked out onto an adjoining piece of land on which someone had planted potatoes. Up and down he walked speaking in tongues on that field! When I came out and saw him, I said, "Lord, take care this man doesn't mash up these people's potatoes." But, as I got into the car, he said, "Reverend, God told me that He'd give you this piece of land to build the church." I asked him, "Who is the owner?" He replied, "I don't know, but this is the land on which God told me you are to build the church." Then I found out that the family that I had just visited owned the land. I went back and said, "Brother, we want to build a church." He said, "Well, I have this piece of land for my son to build his house on, but if you want to build a church I will give it to you." We have a big church there right now.

"Do you think God is going to hear me?"

In that same revival they told me that a man was sick and would like me to go and pray for him. So, I went up into the house and I saw the man lying there. I said, "Brother, I heard you are sick and I've come to pray for you." The man started to cry. He asked, "Do you think God is going to hear me?" So I replied, "Why not? Why shouldn't He hear you?" Then he told me all he had done— how he had paid people to kill other people and he elaborated on other terrible things he had done. So, I told him, "Listen, you did that in your ignorance. If you take Jesus, He will wipe your slate clean and heal you and raise you up." After I prayed for him, I went on to the revival meeting. Later that same night the man came to the revival. He had been healed and raised up.

Tremendous things were happening, tremendous things. At one point, the brethren at my home church felt I was going too fast; they did not want me to go into the different villages and preach the gospel. They thought that I should stay at the local church. So, they decided to take away part of my pay. That month they gave me $20.00 for my month's salary. (This was about 1968–1970.) I said to myself, "I will pour this money out into the hands of God, just like David poured out the water." So, I asked my wife, "Would you go to your mother's and spend a week with her?" She said, "Okay." I gave her $5.00 out of the $20.00. That left me with $15.00. The brother from Grenada who was with me at the founding of the Gasparillo church was there with me. I said, "I want you to go to a town called Siparia." [*It is a town about forty miles southwest of the Princes Town area where Peter lived.*] I said, "Go down there and look for a place for me to preach. I will drive there tonight. When you find the right place, stand out on the pavement, and wave at me when I come by. I gave him $5.00. I was now left with the remaining $10.00.

...the power of God hit that woman...she stood up, healed

That night I started out from home, and spoke in tongues [all the way] until I reached Siparia. As I arrived there, he waved, and I turned in. The power and the presence of God were all over me. When he came to open the car door, he realized I was under the strong influence of the presence of God, so he backed off. After a while I got out. He said, "Reverend, we got this little garage here for you to preach in, but the woman upstairs...they sent her home from the hospital to die. They said that there is nothing that they can do. So, she's upstairs lying on a cot." I went up and I looked at the woman. I had to look twice; I could not fathom what I saw. She was just like skin and bones. I didn't ask her a word; I just laid my hands on her and prayed. Immediately the power of God hit that woman and threw her onto the floor. She stood up, healed! The next day she was washing clothes as though she had never been sick. That clear sign of God's presence caused the revival to spread in that place!

As he reached home, in his kitchen, he became crippled

Seventeen nights of preaching! They gave me a dollar or two to put gas in my car. That night a man came into the revival and started to make noise. He disturbed the meeting, so I took the microphone and I said, "You noisome pestilence, I rebuke you in the name of Jesus." The man ran home. As he reached home, in his kitchen, he became crippled.

The next night his son brought him in the car and put him down at my feet. I told him, "Listen!" (I think he was a Hindu—they worship the leader.) "You don't have to worship me." The son replied, "My father came to disturb your meeting; when he got home last night he suddenly became crippled. So we brought him here that you might pray for him and forgive him." I spoke to the father: "If you will turn to the Lord and ask Him to forgive you, He *will* forgive you, and He will heal you—He will save you." He responded, "I'll do anything, Father, just pray for me." I prayed for him and immediately God raised him up, healed.

> *A similar incident took place during the ministry of the apostle Paul when he was ministering on the Island of Cyprus:*
>
> But Elymas the sorcerer (for that is what his name means) opposed them and tried to turn the proconsul from the faith. Then Saul, who was also called Paul, filled with the Holy Spirit, looked straight at

Elymas and said, "You are a child of the devil and an enemy of everything that is right! You are full of all kinds of deceit and trickery. Will you never stop perverting the right ways of the Lord? Now the hand of the Lord is against you. You are going to be blind, and for a time you will be unable to see the light of the sun." Immediately mist and darkness came over him, and he groped about, seeking someone to lead him by the hand. When the proconsul saw what had happened, he believed, for he was amazed at the teaching about the Lord.

—ACTS 13:8–12

"Let us build a church."

As that [particular] revival was drawing to a close, I felt the Spirit's call to the island of Saint Vincent. Before I could leave, however, the brothers at Siparia approached me with a valid concern. They said, "If you leave here now, when you come back this work will no longer remain because we will have nowhere to worship. The people whose place we are using might put us out. Let us build a church."

"Where is the money," I asked, "and where is the land? Go along," I said, "and look for an empty piece of land; when you find it come and tell me." So they went to a street where they saw a lot of empty land. They reported back. I said, "Go and march around that land seven times and say, 'In the name of Jesus I claim it.'" They came back again; they said they had done what I told them.

I then learned that the owner of the land was the same lady who God healed the day we arrived. So I mused— she is still alive! I went to her with this request: "Sister M, listen. We need to build a church here but we don't have land. We noticed that you have a piece of land. Could you sell it to us?"

She said, "Reverend, the Open Bible church came and offered me five thousand dollars for that land, but I kept it for my grandson. But, you see, after what God did for me, I'll give you the land." So she gave me the land. I said, "All right, Sister M, thank you."

Now we have the place to build the church…but where is the money? A brother in that new congregation was working at a sawmill at the time. He came to me with an offer: "Reverend, I will take all the lumber you need to build the building, and I will pay for it in installments." Another brother said he had bought some sheets of galvanized steel to roof over his house. He said, "I will give you all the galvanized material." I [then] wrote Gordon Lindsay[1] in the United States of America. In those days he was giving $250.00 (U.S.) grants to native churches; he sent us that amount. We built the church with that money, the donated materials, and some other small contributions. The church in Siparia is still standing. (We eventually rebuilt the church: a $250,000 concrete structure. I could go on and tell you a number of stories like that.)

Chapter 4
THE MIRACLE OF SAINT VINCENT
More of Peter's Personal Account

B Y NOW WE had established a church in Grenada. It was from there that the brother (a Grenadian police officer) who helped start the churches in Gasparillo and Siparia had come. When he returned to Grenada, I told him to start another work. He did so, and we sent a young pastor from here to help him. Two weeks later I heard that he told this young pastor, "Don't get back into the pulpit." The young pastor called and told me what had happened. I decided to go see what the problem really was.

...the power of God just broke out in that place—revival—revival!

By the time I reached there, this young pastor had locked up his house and had gone into another town. I stayed outside until about four o'clock in the afternoon. When four o'clock had come and he had not arrived, I broke his window and went in. I decided to stay until he returned. I waited until the next evening, and he still had not returned. So, I asked the neighbor, "Would you allow me to preach some meetings in your yard?" She said, "Of course." So, I started some meetings there and the power of God just broke out in that place—revival—revival!

"When Small Things Fall in the Hands of a Big God, They Become Mighty"

There was a tent set up nearby by a Christian group representing a highly legalistic, dispensational and cessationist[1] denomination; they were hosting a missionary from the States. But, I did not know about that when I started the meetings in this woman's yard. People from that group began to show up at our meetings. Their missionary came and told them, "Listen to me, I do not want you all to go and listen to what is being preached at that meeting; that is false business." So they told him, "You should not condemn the preacher except you listen to him. Go and listen to him and then come back and tell us where he is wrong." That night he came; the presence of God was very evident in the place. The man went back home after the meeting, fell on the floor, and began to cry to God in repentance. God filled him with the Holy Ghost right there. While he was speaking in tongues, the elders called headquarters and told them what had happened to him. They got him on the phone and told him to pack up his grip and return to the States right away. So he left, and a local minister from that organization was sent to take charge.

When he came, he said, "I do not want to hear anything. Nobody is going to that meeting. Do not go and listen to that soapbox preacher." But the people said the same thing to that man. They said, "Go and listen to him one night and then come and tell us what is wrong." When he came into our meeting, he came to find fault; but the presence of God was so strong in the place that he went home. He had an aunt who was a Pentecostal. He took a bus and went to see her. He told her, "I want to get filled with the Holy Ghost." So he got filled with the Holy Spirit and didn't come back to the church.

They sent a third preacher. When the third preacher came, he said, "Where are all the benches from the tent?" They said, "All the benches have gone up to the revival. So he came to see about the benches. That night I was preaching on the five loaves; the title was "When Small Things Fall in the Hands of a Big God, They Become Mighty." I later heard them say, "This man wept… *wept* as he listened to the message."

…you need to put yourself in the hands of God

As I lay in bed the next morning, enjoying the peace and quiet, I thought, "If only I could get up in the morning without somebody rapping on my door." Almost immediately the sister in whose house I was staying called, "Somebody else has come to see you." I opened the door, but did not recognize the man. He said, "Listen, last night I heard you preach. I am a mason by trade. I brought all my tools to put into the hands of God. I want you to pray for that." I said, "It's not the tools you need to put in the hands of God, you need to put yourself in the hands of God." The next night he came and was filled with the Holy Ghost. Meanwhile the other group took down their tent and left. What was the overall result? A number of people got saved and filled with the Holy Ghost, so we decided that we had to build a church there.

Any time you are walking in obedience to God's will you can expect trouble. The local Catholic Church reported that a church was being built without proper approvals. So, the government housing and building association made me take up the concrete I had mixed there. They said they did not want it used there. So I asked this Grenadian brother, "Is there a judge here?" He said, "No, we don't have a judge. The judge comes from Trinidad; we have a magistrate." So,

I said that I would like to speak to him. He took me right to the magistrate's home, and I told him the situation. The magistrate then told me, "It is not the building association that's against you, it is the whole Catholic Church; but I'm giving you the authority to go build your church." He called the building department and told them, "I am giving this man the privilege to go and build." The next morning they returned the approved plan to build the church. Because of all the approval delays, I went to another area and held a revival; God broke through in that revival! We actually built a church at that second location, and then came back and built the church we had started first. The ways of the Lord confound the wisdom of man—two churches!

"My son, rise, and go to St. Vincent. Rise and go to St. Vincent."

During the dedication of this church, I'd preach every night and people would come and give their lives to Christ. But, as I came to pray for the people, all I was hearing was, "My son, rise, and go to St. Vincent. Rise and go to St. Vincent." I mentioned this to the pastor. I said to him, "Listen to me, I am hearing this voice every time I come forward to pray for the people."

> *How very similar this is to the Spirit's working in the life of the apostle Paul. As reported in the sixteenth chapter of the Book of Acts, Paul was proceeding northwest on his Second Missionary Journey from his headquarters at the church in Antioch at the eastern end of the Mediterranean. He planned to head for the province of Asia in the western part of Asia Minor. The Lord had other plans in mind:*

During the night Paul had a vision of a man of Macedonia standing and begging him, "Come over to Macedonia and help us." After Paul had seen the vision, we got ready at once to leave for Macedonia, concluding that God had called us to preach the gospel to them.

—ACTS 16:9–10

...maybe God wants you to go to St. Vincent

The pastor responded: "Well, maybe God wants you to go to St. Vincent." I replied, "I don't know St. Vincent, and I don't know anybody in St. Vincent. Nobody invited me to St. Vincent." He said, "Well, maybe at the service tomorrow night you can ask if anyone knows of someone as a contact in St. Vincent."

So I stood up the following night, and said, "Listen to me, brethren. I would like to have the name and address from somebody in St. Vincent. I believe God is calling me to St. Vincent. If you have such I'd like to have it please."

A brother stood up. He said, "Twenty-five years ago I went to school in St. Vincent, and I had a friend by the name of Mr. T who lived in Edinburgh. But I haven't heard from him since. I don't know if he's alive or dead." I wrote down that name: *Mr. T*, and the location: *Edinburgh*. After that week of revival, the young pastor we had sent from Trinidad and I got into a boat and went to St. Vincent. When we got off the boat, I asked the taxi driver if he knew Edinburgh.

He said, "Yes."

I said, "Do you know of a Mr. T."

He said, "No."

I said, "Well, drive us to Edinburgh."

He was driving up a very steep hill and there were about two houses on that stretch. Suddenly, the Holy Spirit told me we should get off right here. So I told the taxi driver to stop here and put us down.

"No," he said, "the village is over the hill."

"No," I replied, "I think God wants me to stay here. Let us off!" So, he put down our luggage by the roadside. I just stood there. Just then I saw a man coming down the hill toward us. I walked over to him and said, "Good Morning, Sir."

"Good Morning."

"Do you know Mr. Mr. T?" He smiled. I repeated myself, "Mr. T; do you know him?

"I am Mr. T."

"Well, we are missionaries from Trinidad."

"Wait, I am not a Christian; but my neighbor is a Christian."

He took me over to meet the neighbor. I said, "We are missionaries from Trinidad; we have been to Grenada, and now we have been called to St. Vincent."

She said, "Wait a minute." She called a Salvation Army captain from the kitchen. She said, "Carmen, come and tell these men what I told you yesterday."

He said, "Yesterday, you told me to fix up the room, and that two men, two missionaries, will come and stay there."

That night we walked out into the town, and saw a lot of people, but I had no inspiration to preach. So, I told my young preacher friend, "Well, you better preach." He said, "No, you are the preacher. I will sing." Then we returned to the home we were staying in.

The following morning the lady we were staying with told us of a friend of hers who was sick. So we went to her home near the airport and prayed for her. After praying for her we just sat there without any real [sense of what to do next]. After awhile my friend said, "Reverend, it's getting

So, I told my friend, "We are going to preach here. We're going to preach down here." But we didn't have any money. All I had was $45. That was all the money we had together. (This was about 1968–1970.) [Regardless], I went down into the city to an electronic store, and asked the owner, "Could you rent us a PA set and a tape recorder? I don't have the money to pay you now, but after the revival I will pay you."

He said, "Reverend, take whatever you want in the store and go ahead."

...and while she was going home her ears opened up

So we took the PA set and the tape recorder with some music—some gospel songs— and returned to the little place where we were staying. I went into the little house and shut myself up there. I began to pray to God. I said to my friend, "You go and set up the mike, and play the music." At seven o'clock I came out, and I saw about 200 people. I preached that night, and I prayed a mass prayer. A deaf woman was attending the meeting, and while she was going home her ears opened up. However, we were not aware of anything of this nature happening.

The next day at the market we overheard people discussing an evangelistic service that had taken place the night before. They were also talking about a deaf woman who had miraculously received her hearing there. I know that I did not pray for any deaf woman at our service, so I thought, "I wonder whose meeting?"

When we returned the next night, the attendance had grown to about 800 people and the revival really started. When we finally ended the series of services, attendance had reached about 4,000. They came with cars and trucks; they climbed up on houses and on trees to catch a glimpse of what was happening. The power of God was just sweeping the place. We saw how the mighty power of God can move in spite of persecution and through any obstacle.

> *One evening in 1980 the author sat at a hotel restaurant table in Toronto with a small group of ministers listening to German evangelist, Reinhard Bonnke, describe the events leading up to his great work on the continent of Africa. The story he told was exciting and reminds me of what happened to Peter. Brother Bonnke was touring through southern Africa looking for evangelistic opportunities at churches. When he arrived at a particular town one day, the Lord seemed to tell him to rent the stadium there. After some reluctance, he went to the municipal offices and rented the stadium. When he began the services, he preached to a disappointingly small group. But, about halfway into his message, without any apparent initiation on his part, people in the congregation began to be miraculously healed. The next night the stadium was packed. This was the beginning of his now famous crusades through Africa with hundreds of thousands coming to Christ.*

...the presence of God

I took up one offering, $182.00 and a penny, and I was able to pay the man for his equipment. We baptized a number of people and built a church. The church is standing there, along with our Bible school, today. And as a result of that, we have four other churches in St. Vincent. The answer: the presence of God! (That church is International Pentecostal Assemblies—Foursquare affiliate.)

To obey is better than sacrifice, and to heed is better
than the fat of rams.

—1 Samuel 15:22

One of the persons being baptized amidst great joy was
a teacher at the Methodist school. But her father, who had
been pleasantly anticipating his daughter's soon promotion,
saw the baptism as the death of her (and his) dreams. He
was so upset and angry that he came early one morning to
the house where my partner and I were staying. He started
to ridicule and curse us, and said that his daughter did
not know what she was doing. This went on for about an
hour. I remained in my room, praying. Finally, I opened
the window and looked out at him. I said, "Sir, you are just
a noisome pestilence, and, in the name of Jesus Christ, I
rebuke this noisome pestilence." Immediately, the man left
and walked away. He had not gone more than a distance of
300 feet when he fell to the ground, crippled. Some of the
people nearby came and carried him home. When I heard
of the incident, I told my friend to go and pray for him and
to tell him that he had grieved the Holy Spirit and should
repent. He told the man that if he were to repent, the Lord
would forgive him and raise him up. But the man said, "I
was born a Methodist and I want to die a Methodist." So, in
seven days he died and was buried.

Chapter 5
BUILDING GOD'S CHURCH

AN INTRODUCTION BY PETER'S SON, JOSHUA

...those early church members gave out of their poverty

As congregations of new believers began to form about the island, shelters were required in which to meet. The members were mostly poor farmers. Nevertheless, they loved the Lord and wanted to see a "house of God" built in their communities. Whatever they had they would gladly donate so that the church building could be built. For instance, they would give their iron, chrome, or brass bedsprings and bed heads to be used as reinforcement in the concrete walls or floors. The extent to which those early church members gave out of their poverty is now brilliantly coming to light. In order to make way for current expansion needs we must demolish many of the older structures. We are discovering bedsprings and truck chassis, and our hearts are melting. Tears spring up in my eyes when I realize where we have come from and how these saints of God used what they had to perfect the "house of God."

Men that worked in the sawmills would pledge their entire week's salary to the sawmill owner in return for lumber to be used in the building projects. They would bring the lumber, and then build the churches themselves. My dad would come down from the pulpit, roll up his sleeves, and join them as they went about their labor of love. He was always at home with a shovel and pick, hammer and saw, as he pitched in, from footing to finish work. He would be there to give encouragement and to put in labor with the other men. He was one of them.

One day a man came looking for my dad. "Where is the pastor?" My dad just happened to be down in the mud digging a foundation. He answered, "I am the pastor." The man was touched by the "servant's attitude" of my father. He could not believe that the pastor of a church would be down in a hole, all muddied up. He was touched by my dad's humble manner and that alone caused him to be won to Jesus Christ. He saw servanthood lived out.

In those early days of my father's ministry, he would go up into the mountains with some of the brethren; they would cross ravines and lagoons. They would fell trees, and drag them out by hand. Two on one side and one on the other, they would drag these trees, sometimes for miles, to get them out of the forest in order to make the lumber they needed for benches and the pulpit. We still have a few pieces of that original furniture.

PETER CONTINUES HIS TESTIMONY

...he had spent a week sharpening it

During the time I was pastoring in Cumuto, an incident occurred regarding a Hindu woman who had just been saved and who wanted to "follow the Lord in water baptism." Her husband, also a Hindu, protested strongly. Nevertheless, the woman insisted that in spite of her husband's objections, she intended to obey the ordinance of the Lord. So the man went and bought himself a machete and decided to kill both of us on the day of the baptism. We later learned that he had spent a week sharpening it.

On the Sunday morning of the baptism the woman arrived and went in. The husband also arrived and stood right outside the front door. (Word had gotten out of the man's intentions, so most of the members stayed home that day.)

I preached the message that morning, and I asked the wife if she was ready to get baptized. She said, "Yes, Pastor, I'm ready to be baptized." The man lifted the cutlass, waiting for us to pass in front of him. I came down from the platform, and I told the woman to follow me. I walked right in front of him as he stood with his cutlass raised, the woman following behind me right out the front door. We both went down into the font and I baptized her. As we came up out of the water, the man left and went home. Two weeks after that the man gave his heart to the Lord. Right after this he went with me into the forest to cut down timber to use for benches in the church and to build a new church, we even spent a night together in the forest getting the logs out.

...near the place where Columbus landed

The Lord called me to go into the village of Basse Terre-Moruga, near the place where Columbus landed on the south coast of Trinidad. The week before I went there some of the residents had chased out a Christian who had gone there to preach. Because of this, the people of my church warned me that I should not go there and that the locals were very dangerous. But I told them that God had impressed upon my mind to go to Basse Terre to preach, so I must go.

We rented a hall that just happened to be across the road

from a rum shop (bar) with a jukebox. We set up our sound system, and that evening began the service. The owner of the bar turned up the volume on the jukebox to its maximum. So, I sent one of the brothers to ask the proprietor if he would lower the volume. I told him to tell the owner that in a little while we will be finished and then he could turn up his jukebox as much as he desires. The man sent back his reply: "Go and tell that preacher to go and do his business; I am doing mine."

When I got that word something stirred in my heart. I took the mike and said, "[You] noisome pestilence; in the name of Jesus Christ of Nazareth, I rebuke you." As the words left my mouth the jukebox caught on fire and burned up. The man closed down his rum shop after that, and up until now the place remains unoccupied.

After the revival that began at that location, a woman came to me and said, "I understand you want a piece of land to build a church."

I said, "Yes, we are looking for a piece of land." She said, "I have just bought this land for the purpose of building my house here. But, I am going to give you this land on one condition. And I want your promise."

"What is it?" I asked her.

She replied, "Wherever you are in this world when I die, I want you to leave where you are and come here and bury me. If you'll make me that promise, I will give you the land."

I said, "I will do my best. Wherever I am and I hear that you are dead, I will come to attend your funeral and to perform the rites." And so the woman gave us seven lots of land. We built a church on that property and are currently replacing it with a larger, more beautiful structure to accommodate the increased membership.

Maybe tomorrow night you will not be here

During the building of the initial church at Basse Terre-Moruga, I was invited to hold evangelistic meetings in Jeffers. One particular night about seven or eight young men from [a well-known, historically liturgical denomination] were sent to interrupt the service. As I preached, they made noise and certain unkind remarks that disturbed the service. I changed the course of my preaching, and I warned them about the judgment of God. After the service that night as I was passing by one of these young men, he said to me, "You made us frightened tonight, but tomorrow night we will be back."

Perhaps the following (my reply) was inspired: "Maybe tomorrow night you *will not* be here." I left. Very early the next morning that same young man waited by the roadside for transportation to go to work. As he stood there, a truck passed by with a piece of rope dangling from the cargo bed. As it swerved around the curve in the road the rope swung out and somehow hooked him around the neck and dragged him under the vehicle where he was crushed to death. We were horrified when we heard. An incident in the Bible regarding some young boys being mauled by a bear comes to mind (see 2 Kings 2:23–24).

...at the oil fields in Barrackpore

As the result of a cry for help by one of the workers at the Barrackpore oil fields, a great revival broke out and quite a number of people got saved, healed, baptized in water, and filled with the Holy Spirit. A local body of believers was established, and we built a little shed to accommodate the people; it served as the church building there for a time until the main facility could be completed.

It is exciting to see how God moves when there are hearts hungry for His salvation, hearts broken by the pain and embarrassment of human failure. One day during lunch break at the oil fields in Barrackpore, a neighbor of Peter's, perhaps empathizing with a co-worker's struggle with alcohol, suggested that he ought to hear Peter's clear presentation of the gospel. The co-worker, an elder in the Presbyterian Church in the vicinity of Monkey Town, became excited at the prospect. He said, "If you invite him down, I will invite all the people." So the arrangements were made, and Peter went onto the school compound there to start preaching. Hundreds of people came out and the presence of God was evident. One night there was so much rain that the road to the compound was flooded. In spite of the horrid conditions, about seventeen women, carrying flambeaus (bottles of kerosene with wicks) and skirts lifted above their knees, were seen coming through two foot deep water just to hear the Word. God healed people...delivered people. Many were saved. Revival broke out. In time a beautiful church was built there.

...healed by the power of God

One of the sisters there had a boil on her leg. Her friends tried to persuade her to go to the doctor, but she said, "When my pastor comes on Sunday afternoon, he will pray for me and I believe I will be healed." So she suffered through the week. On Sunday I went to visit her. By now the fever was quite high and the boil quite painful. I laid my hands on her, prayed, and asked the Lord to heal her and to remove the affliction. Just as I left the room the boil burst and its contents came out with such a force that it splashed on the wall. The people in the house that day saw her rise from her bed, healed by the power of God.

Chapter 6
SPIRITUAL WARFARE

Peter Continues His Story

...frightening demonic manifestations

There is a Hindu family about half a mile down the road from my home here in Indian Walk. One day something strange began to happen. The family members began to experience frightening demonic manifestations in their home. They would hear voices calling; they saw their oil lamp (they do not have electricity in that area) being lit, lifting off the wall bracket, and floating in the air. They saw the lamp move from the wall and settle on the table. The kitchen stove would suddenly light without anyone touching it. The tables would move from one location to another. Then the demon behind this manifestation began to slap the husband and his wife; you could actually see the welts from the fingers on their faces.

Strange, illogical thoughts of suicide invaded the minds of the members of that family. At one point the wife became so overcome by a devilish fit of anger toward her husband that she experienced the urge to kill both him and herself. The children got so scared that they would not stay at home. They left and went over to their grandmother's. The *thing* seemed to crawl under her bed; and in a clear voice, said to the woman, "I'm going to destroy you. I will kill you and your husband." The family got so frustrated, they did not know exactly what to do. They called in the local Hindu priest. He came, dug into his own bag of occult tricks, and performed some ceremonial services for them, all to no avail. In fact, he was accosted by the demonic personalities as well. Under demonic influence, family members uttered, "No priest can kick them out." Every conceivable source of help was pursued—obeah men, witch doctors, all to no avail.

One day the man's brother came and suggested, "Why don't you go to Rev. Hosein? He lives right near here. He's a preacher. Why not go and ask him to pray for you." So, the man came up to my home one afternoon, related the circumstances, and asked me to pray for him. I invited him in, and I led him to Christ. I said, "You need to accept Jesus Christ as your Savior and Lord." He did.

Then I told him, "Tomorrow evening I am coming to your home. I'm going to pray and release your home and your family from all demonic influence." The next evening my wife and I, and my daughter-in-law, Rhea, went to their home and prayed. We rebuked the devil in the name of Jesus Christ, and commanded it to leave the home. That was the last time this demon ever interfered with that family. We had the joy and the privilege of baptizing the entire family. They are serving the Lord in the church today. As a result of the miracle, the man's eighty-year-old mother, the matriarch of the home, was saved. She had been on her deathbed and was healed of terminal cancer by God's miraculous power. The power of God is a reality. The entire family had been practicing Hindus.

...dance barefooted on live coals

There was a renowned obeah man, a witch doctor that lived here in Indian Walk; his name was Papa Z [name withheld]. People came to him from all over the West

Indies. He was the spiritual leader of the occultist Orisha Shango religion, which originated in Africa, and was brought here by the African slaves. He was also a minister of the local Shango Baptist "church." At first the government of Trinidad and Tobago banned the group because they believed it to be occult. Nevertheless, a number of people continued to practice that religion covertly.

Part of the ritual of this religion is an annual feast during which the followers dance and shout and offer sacrifices. I decided to attend one night just to see what was going on. That night a goat was brought into the midst of the congregation and its head swiped off with a machete. Papa Z, along with his followers, drank the goat's blood as it spurted from the carcass. After that, members of the congregation started to dance barefooted on live coals of fire with absolutely no protection on their feet. They danced for a period of time in about six inches to one foot deep of live coal fire and, seemingly, nothing happened. The authorities were tipped off, and one morning they sent two policemen to apprehend the leader. They sat out in his tent, waiting for him. News came to him that the policemen were there. I do not know what he practiced, but he cast some sort of spell on these policemen, such that they just sat there and were unable to move. They could not get up. When night began to fall, they begged to be set free. Papa Z told them, "Never, ever, come back to interfere with me." They agreed and were released to go.

One day I was preaching at a baptismal service down by the river near here. I took my text from chapter 8 of the Book of Acts, where Philip the evangelist went down to Samaria and preached the gospel. Because of the miraculous supernatural power of God present as Philip preached, the city bowed before the Lord Jesus Christ. There was a man there in Samaria that worked sorcery; his name was Simon, and referred to as a sorcerer [*See Acts 8:9.*] As I preached my message, I made reference to Papa Z, showing that he was just like Simon and that he was bewitching the entire community and, in fact, the nation. While I was preaching, some of the people left the baptismal site and went straight to him and told him what I was saying. He went into his shrine for a while, and then came out. He told the people that in three days there would be a funeral, and that I would be buried.

The baptismal service ended and I went back home. That night a strange thing happened in my room. I felt my bed begin to shake. I thought at first that there had been an earthquake; I got up. The shaking stopped. As I lay back down, the shaking began with a lot more force. I quickly realized that this was not something natural. There must have been some sort of supernatural force entering my room. I read a portion of the Word of God and then went back to sleep. Suddenly I felt my bed floating in the air. I got out and commanded it to go back down. The bed settled itself back on the floor. Then I prayed for about forty-five minutes.

The next day I started to fast and pray. I fasted three days and nights. At the conclusion of the fast, I came out of my house, turned my face toward where Papa Z the obeah man lived, and commanded the evil spirit to return from whence it came. It wasn't long after that he took sick with an unusual disease. All of the veins in his body began to burst and bleed, and he became infested with worms. He died a little later on and was buried right in front of the Shango Baptist church of which he had been general secretary!

This was probably some form of hemorrhagic disorder. We are reminded of the demise of King Herod Antipas (Acts 12:21–23), who received the glory due to God and was eaten by worms.

...his power came from the enemy

He was not a born again Christian, but the people believed that he had a gift from God. In fact, his power came from the enemy, as had been the case with the Samaritan sorcerer, Simon, in the Bible.

"Cursed is the man who carves an image."

In Deuteronomy 27:15, God says, "Cursed is the man who carves an image or casts an idol—a thing detestable to the LORD." All those who practice Hinduism have done just this, either directly or indirectly. One of the elders of our church, Brother S, is a factory owner. His wife is an educator. It seems that his entire family was, for many years, under some sort of devilish curse. One afternoon several years ago—about two o'clock—his younger brother heard a voice saying to him, "Why don't you go and have a swim in the sea." And so he did. He drowned!

Another of his brothers died under similar circumstances. Brother S himself had been driven by demons; he had been a drunkard and gambler. Sometimes we would come home in the morning after a full night of gambling. He became so distraught over his apparently hopeless condition that he visited almost every known obeah man in Trinidad, seeking deliverance. He was very conscious that something evil was controlling him, but no one could help. One day while descending a flight of stairs, he felt some sort of force come against him and throw him down six stairs to the bottom. He was taken to the hospital. Upon his return home, a forest ranger, who supplied some of the lumber for his factory, paid him a visit. Brother S. related to him his plight. The ranger, also a minister of the gospel and member of my church, told him about our ministry and suggested that he ought to come down and see me, certain that he would be helped.

The ranger brought Brother S to my office, and I explained to him that Jesus Christ does not simply want to set him free from his present problems but wants to make him free *permanently*. I explained to him how this is possible should he receive Jesus as Lord and Savior. Recognizing and acknowledging his sinful nature and understanding that he deserved eternal punishment for his sins, he gratefully accepted Jesus as Savior[1] and Master.

I prayed for [Brother S] and commanded the evil force to be broken over his life, and to set him free. He went home, and has been free from that day onward. He was eventually baptized in water and filled with the Holy Spirit. He attended our Bible school, and is presently one of the teachers there. He is also an elder in our church. The power of God is a reality.

One day I visited his home and his little son came out to greet me. When he saw it was me, he went back inside and told his parents, "God has come." He was so inspired by the miracle that took place in his father's life that he thought that I was some sort of great man. Perhaps even like God. Of course, now he knows better. The entire family now worships at our church and they are a real blessing. He built a church and now pastors it.

Chapter 7
GO INTO ALL THE WORLD
More Personal Account from Peter

I lifted up the sweet rice and asked the Lord's blessing upon it in the name of Jesus

During the early years of my life, while my family were still Muslims, it was customary that after reaping a crop of rice the priest (Imam) would come and bless the rice before we ate any of it. It so happened one year, soon after my conversion, that my uncle who was the Imam was not available for that particular ceremony; so I officiated. I lifted up the sweet rice and asked the Lord's blessing upon it in the name of Jesus Christ. We thanked Him for the harvest. We thanked Him for the crop that He had given. And I prayed that the blessing of the Lord would be upon it.

My grandmother was so upset that I did not pray to Allah that she told my mother that Allah would be angry with us. That night at midnight she came to our house crying and said that Allah had slapped her on both sides of her face and that we are responsible because we did not bless the rice or dedicate the rice in the name of Allah. So, I told my grandmother, "If this is so, then perhaps there was an injustice, because I am the one responsible for not blessing the rice in the name of Allah; why should you be slapped? I am the one who should be slapped." So, my grandmother walked out of the house and left. With that an even more personal, more painful form of persecution came upon my life. But, I continued steadfastly in the name of Jesus Christ and worshipped and called upon that name.

During the course of my silent prayer the headache left

I remember one day when my mother was suffering severely with a headache. I was not at home. I had gone to my elder brother's home to spend the day. When I arrived home late in the afternoon, my mother said, "Where were you all this time? I have been suffering with this headache, and I have longed to see you."

I thought to myself, "My other brothers are here, my sisters are here, why should my mother long for me?" So, I gently laid my hands on her, and asked the Lord Jesus Christ to touch her and remove the pain. During the course of my silent prayer the headache left.

My mother asked, "What did you put upon my head."

I said, "I just called on the name of Jesus."

She said, "The headache is gone." We give God praise for manifesting Himself to my mother and to the rest of my family. Praise the Lord!

The author's mother-in-law had regularly suffered from migraine headaches. One morning as my wife and I arrived at her home for breakfast, she met us at the door in considerable agony. It suddenly occurred to us that she should not have to suffer this way. We prayed for her on the spot in the name of Jesus Christ of Nazareth. The headache left instantly; she never experienced a migraine again.

It should be noted that God does not restrict the use of His spiritual gifts to a certain select few who are members of an elite priestly class, but uses any truly submitted, Spirit-filled believer who is available and ready to obey. (See 1 Corinthians 12:7–11.)

"I will lead you into *shepherd's rest* and there I shall manifest My power."

Now, I was praying in my room one afternoon, a number of years after this last incident, between the hours of two and three o'clock. The word of the Lord came to me through prophecy in 1975:

> My son, thou shall arise and go among a people whom you know not, a people that I will send you to; and I will manifest My power and show forth My glory among them that they will know of a truth, I am the Lord God, and you are My servant. And I will lead you into *shepherd's rest*, and there I shall manifest My power.

Well, my first thought was that this word from God meant that I was being prepared for my death. So, I came out of the room and met with my son, Joshua, and said to him,

"The Lord has just spoken to me and I believe He's calling me home.

"Why is that? Are you sick or something?"

"No, I'm not sick," I said. Then I shared the prophecy with him.

After consideration, he replied: "Maybe that prophesy doesn't mean that."

Two weeks later, I received a letter from Rev. Sidney Fontenot from Sulfur, Louisiana, inviting me to speak at a Full Gospel Businessmen's Fellowship International convention in nearby Jennings. I went there and spoke. A Roman Catholic priest, Father M, attended the event. After the service, he approached me and invited me to his church. He said, "I would like you to say the same thing you said here, to my people."

I did not understand him at the moment because of his southern accent. So I said to him, "Praise the Lord." I thought he meant, simply, that what I had said here would be a blessing to his people. I said, "Praise the Lord. Let us give God the glory."

But my friend, Rev. Fontenot said, "He is asking you to come to his church and preach just as you preached here." So I asked Rev. Fontenot if he would go with me. He replied, "No. He doesn't want anyone to come with you. He wants you to come to his church alone."

"Well," I said, "I have never been in a Catholic Church before."

He said, "Never mind, you go—go along with him." So, I went and preached in that Catholic Church in Welch, Louisiana. I preached on the subject of what it means to be born again. That night eighty-four persons came forward and gave their lives to Christ.

This anointing is available to all that believe

The priest told me that he had called Rev. Fontenot and requested that I would come and spend the night with him. That night the priest filled two tapes asking me questions about the anointing of God, the power of God, and the Spirit of the Lord. And he asked me, "Is it possible for me to have this anointing that is upon you?"

I said, "This anointing is available to all that believe, 'for the promise is unto you, and to your children, and to all that are far off, even as many as the LORD our God shall call'" (Acts 2:39, KJV). That night, about midnight, he received the baptism of the Holy Spirit. Early the next morning he called six of his people, and they all received the baptism of the Holy Spirit.

I continued there with him for a week. On that Thursday night he asked many of the nuns in that area to come for a special meeting. I cannot say exactly how many received, but quite a number of nuns received the baptism of the Holy Spirit. I later heard that he resigned his church and went as an evangelist in the Charismatic Movement.

> *The Catholic Charismatic Movement began about 1967 at Duquesne University when a number of Catholic clergy read David Wilkerson's book* The Cross and the Switchblade. *As a result of this, many in the Roman Church experienced the Pentecostal baptism with the evidence of speaking in tongues and other gifts of the Spirit such as prophecy, healings, and miracles.*

Call off the... meeting

Well, I went back to Sulfur after those meetings, and the Rev. Fontenot told me that he had a week of revival meetings lined up for me. The first night back I preached. As the meeting closed he said we were going to call off the following night's meeting. He said, "I have no justifiable reason for it, but I just feel the Lord would want me to close off the meeting tomorrow night. We are going to continue the meetings the night after." There were some brethren in the service that night that had come from another area. Knowing that I would not be preaching the following night, they asked would I go with them. They were having some meetings, and they would like me to visit with them. So, I asked the Reverend if it was okay, and he said, "Sure, go ahead." And so, they drove me to their place.

I noticed there was a big sign saying "Shepherd's Rest"

As they turned the corner to go into the gate where the meetings were being held, I noticed there was a big sign saying "Shepherd's Rest." Then I remembered the prophecy: the Lord had said, "I will send you into 'shepherd's rest.'" As the meeting began, we were sitting on the floor. Each person was sharing a little. It came time for me to share. I spoke about five minutes and sat down. Then the Word of the Lord came to me saying, "Son, thou shall arise and speak to this people all the words that I will put in thy mouth."

So I said, "Lord, I do not know the situation of the meetings here. I would not like to intrude. If you want me to speak, ask somebody to invite me to speak."

Before I was finished speaking to the Lord, a woman stood up and said, "This is the first night I have come into your meetings, but I believe the Lord would have Rev. Hosein to speak to us again." They all agreed, so I stood up and spoke for about fifteen minutes, and then made an altar call.

All of the people in the room responded. So I said, "Those who need prayers for their bodies come to my left, those that need salvation stand in front of me, and those that need the baptism of the Holy Spirit line up on my right. The first person I prayed for was the rodeo queen of Louisiana. She went under the power of God, speaking in tongues. The second person was the president of the rodeo club; he received the baptism of the Holy Spirit. Great miracles took place. We continued the meeting there for awhile and the Lord really showed forth His power and glory just as He had said to me, "I will lead you into Shepherd's Rest and there I will show forth My glory and My power." After those meetings I went back to Sulfur.

While I was preaching there a missionary came in one night and said, "Listen, we are having a convention in Canada. Would you go along with us?" And I said, "Sure, but I don't have the money for the ticket." He said that the church would raise the money. So I went to Canada.

While I was in Canada at a convention, there were some brethren that said, "Listen, we are having a convention in London. Would you go along with us?" I said, "I am available, but I don't have a ticket." They said, "We will take care of that." So, we went on to London.

> As you go, preach this message: "The kingdom of heaven is near." Heal the sick, raise the dead, cleanse those who have leprosy, drive out demons. Freely you have received, freely give. Do not take along any gold or silver or copper in your belts; take no bag for the journey, or extra tunic, or sandals or a staff; for the worker is worth his keep.
>
> —MATTHEW 10:7–10

So, we went to London

While I was on that plane I sat near a gentleman who was chewing tobacco and spitting it into a glass. I pleaded: "Lord, why should you want me to sit near a man who is chewing tobacco? And, furthermore, I have to preach in a convention tomorrow." So I stood up and looked for a vacant seat.

The Lord said to me, "I want you to sit right here." As I sat down the compassion of the Lord came over me.

I looked at this man, and I said, "Sir, it looks like you are suffering."

He said, "Yes, I can hardly breathe. I have to keep chewing this tobacco."

I said, "Well, I am a minister of the gospel. Would you mind if I prayed for you?"

He said, "I would love that."

So, while sitting alongside him, I laid my hands on him and commanded, in the name of Jesus, that the yoke be destroyed and that he would be loosed from his sickness. Instantly he was healed and delivered. I noticed that he was dressed in an unusual garment, so I asked him, "What is the meaning of all these stripes?"

He said, "I am a diplomat, and I wear this clothing (probably a diplomatic sash) so that when I go to immigration I can go right through. I don't have to be checked like the other people. I am a Canadian. And, if anytime you come to Canada you can come to my home; I would love to have you there." Before we finally departed, he gave me some money, and he went his way. I went mine.

For a similar event in the Bible, please read about Phillip the evangelist and the Ethiopian government official: Acts 8:26–40.

The next night we went to the convention in London. There were about a dozen preachers on the platform. Each one would preach one night. They asked me to share a little as a visitor. As I spoke, I saw all of the preachers leave the platform and go aside. So I thought maybe they had a problem with my theology. Then, in a little while they came back. What they went to discuss was that they would give up their night of preaching and allow me to speak all through the convention. God really blessed us in that convention. Then they asked me to go to Scotland. So I've been to Scotland—I spent a little time there. While there I was told of a convention soon to be held in Wales. They asked if I would go. I said, "Sure, I will go."

The convention was held at Evan Roberts' church in Wales

The convention was held at Evan Roberts' church in Wales. The church was packed out, and I happened to be the guest speaker that day. After preaching, I gave an altar call. People knelt from outside the church near the road, straight up to the platform. Three aisles were filled with people. The conference director told me that a bus would be coming for us at six, so we would have to hurry up with the service. I immediately informed him, "The bus will not come at six; the bus will come at seven. So, let us take our time and deal with these people; pray with them."

> *Peter's statement was not arbitrary, nor a guess, but the speaking forth of a gift of knowledge (see 1 Corinthians 12:8). See also John 4:17, where Jesus spoke truth to the Samaritan woman.*

We prayed for the people and led many of them to Christ; we had a great service. When it was seven o'clock the bus showed up and we all went back to London.

> *Evan Roberts was saved in a revival that broke out in a church at New Quay on the Bay of Cardigan, Wales, in 1903. The revival only lasted about a year, but had a major impact on the spiritual life of all of Wales. It was reported that the pubs and the jail cells were emptied and that the mules in the mines could no longer understand the miners whose vocabularies were suddenly cleansed of profanity. The revival was considered by many as the primary forerunner of the great*

Pentecostal revival that broke out at the Azusa Street mission in Los Angeles in 1906 and began one of the greatest moves of the Spirit in modern times. From this came such fellowships as the Assemblies of God, the various Church of God groups, the Foursquare Church, the Elim Pentecostal Church, the Apostolic Church, and many other Pentecostal denominations.

I flew to California and preached in Bishop Crouch's church

From London I flew to California and preached in Bishop Crouch's church. I think he was the chief bishop for the Church of God in Christ at the time; he was also the father of the well-known Christian singer, Andre Crouch. From there I went down to Tijuana, Mexico, and had a week of revival services. God poured His Spirit upon us in Tijuana. After that I went back to California. I preached in a few states, and then came back to Trinidad.

I lived to see what God had spoken in that room fulfilled! He had said He would lead me "to a people whom you know not, and I will...show forth my glory among them...and...into *shepherd's rest.*" So the word, His Word, was fulfilled. I give God praise that the Spirit of God can lead us as we open our hearts to Him.

Chapter 8
HOME AGAIN

Peter Story Continues

Back in Princes Town

There are some other miracles that I would like to mention that might interest you. There was a very rich woman in Princes Town. Her husband had dealt with the occult. After he died, this woman got very ill. She had two daughters who were medical specialists in the United States of America, so she went there many times to visit them. But, she grew worse.

She came back and then went to Guyana seeking help. From there she went to Suriname. Then, she was referred back to the States and from there to London, where she got baptized. She was no better. They suggested that she should go down to France. So she went to France seeking help, and from France she went to India. They told her if she dipped in the Ganges she would be healed. So she went and was dipped in the Ganges several times and even brought back a bottle of water from the Ganges. But, she came back home ready to die. She had given up all hope.

While lying in the bed, she prayed in her heart, "Lord, I have traveled to so many countries of the world seeking help but there is no help. Would you send someone that can help me?" She prayed this prayer for about a week. "Send someone to help me."

...about 4:00 that afternoon a man came and stood at my gate

I had been fasting for ten days and nights at home, and about 4:00 that afternoon a man came and stood at my gate and told me that a Mistress R in Princes Town would like to see me. She is sick. I was feeling very weak in my body from the fast, so I told the man that I did not know Mrs. R, and I did not know where she lived. He gave me directions. I should go around the back of her house, behind the icebox, and I would find a little gateway that leads into her parlor, and on into her home.

I said to the man, "Listen, tell her I will come tomorrow afternoon."

The man looked at me and said, "Not tomorrow, it must be this evening," and he left.

So I went down to Princes Town, following his directions. I went into the parlor and I met a girl. I asked, "Is Mistress R here?" She said, "Yes, but she is sick, and she cannot get out of bed." I told her, "Go and tell her that the preacher she sent for is here." The girl came back and told me that Mistress R did not send for a preacher; nevertheless, she would like to see me.

What! Could that man that came to Peter's gate have been another angel?

Do not forget to show hospitality to strangers, for by so doing some people have shown hospitality to angels without knowing it.

—HEBREWS 13:2

...she was ready to die

I went in and looked at her, and realized that she was so helpless she could not even get out of bed—she was *ready to die.* I read a passage of scripture to her from the Gospel of John: "Let not your heart be troubled: ye believe in God, believe also in me" (John 14:1, KJV). She took a corner of the sheet on the bed and wiped the tears from her eyes. I told her that the Lord was able to heal her and raise her up and that I would like to pray for her.

She said, "Sure, I'd love that."

As I laid my hands upon her the power of God came upon that woman and threw her off the bed—right onto the floor. Then she stood to her feet. The girl saw this from the parlor and ran and hugged her. The Holy Spirit told me to lay hands on both of them. They both went down under the power of God. The woman was perfectly and instantly healed by the power of God.

Before I left she said that stones would fall on this house every night.

> *This was probably a demonic manifestation known as "kinesis." The author ministered to a demonized woman years ago who never really wanted to be free from occult involvement, just the consequences. She regularly experienced things flying around in her room at night. Had she surrendered control of her life to Jesus Christ she would have been completely freed. We pray that she has since come to the Savior; we know that she has heard the clear message of the gospel.*

I...asked God to deliver the home

That house was [apparently] possessed—*demon* possessed. So she asked would I pray for their protection before leaving them. I went outside, lifted up my hands, and asked God to deliver the home. And I charged the devil never to torment the house again, for it is written that no plague shall come near your dwelling (Ps. 91:10, KJV); and I left.

This woman began coming down to my church, but it was really too far for her. So, I referred her to the Open Bible Church. She donated $5,000 to them to buy a piano. The woman lived many years after. She was a wonderful Christian.

"Is this the church where they pray for sick people?"

There was another miracle that took place. I was pastoring a church out in the country where the power of God was moving on people. Many people were healed. A Hindu man heard of these services and rode on his bicycle about eight miles to attend one of them. He met me at the front of the little thatched roof church where we meet and asked, "Is this the church where they pray for sick people?"

I said, "Yes. Are you sick?"

He said, "No, but I left my wife dying at home, and I came to ask you to pray for her."

So I said, "Come in, into the church." As the service progressed I forgot all about what the man had said; but when I stood up to preach, the Holy Spirit brought it back to me. I turned my face toward the direction where this man's wife was located. The man had told me, "I am not sure if I will meet my wife alive when I get back."

So, I prayed for her. I said, "I send the Word of God which says, 'He sent his word, and healed them, and delivered them from their destructions' (Ps.107:20, KJV)." I prayed for the woman—I sent the Word of God to her. And I left it at that.

When the man arrived home that night he saw people gathered in his yard. He thought immediately that his wife had died and that the neighbors had gathered because his little daughter must have spread the word that Mama had died. But, to his surprise, his wife greeted him right at the step as he walked in. He asked her what happened.

She said, "At about 8:30, while I was lying on the bed, a

power came upon me and threw me off the bed." She said, "I stood up and started to cry and our daughter started to cry. It awakened the neighborhood and they all came here. I am healed."

The next day this man came and said, "My wife is healed, Reverend, and I want to give you a piece of land at my place to build a church." But our church was not that far from there so we did not bother with the land. There were mighty signs and wonders.

...my shadow fell across her body

Early one morning, perhaps during the mid 1970s, a woman walked up the street to our home here on Loney Road and asked me to come and pray for her little girl who had suffered all night with an earache and a fever. When I arrived a short time later, the girl was resting in a hammock out in the yard. I can still remember her crying out, "Look, Mama, the Reverend is coming!" As I approached her, my shadow fell across her body.

> As a result, people brought the sick into the streets and laid them on beds and mats so that at least Peter's shadow might fall on some of them as he passed by.
> —Acts 5:15

She later testified that the pain left her at that very moment, and that she was completely healed. As a result of this miracle, the entire family turned to the Lord. She has a family of her own now and regularly worships at our church in Jordan Hill.

One of the girls said, "Mama just died."

One night at about 2:00 in the morning two girls came crying at my gate. My first thought was about those people who have a tendency to put out their children when they accept Christ. So I thought, "Their parents must have driven them out because they have accepted Christ." I came out and asked what the problem was.

One of the girls said, "Mama just died."

So I got in my car and I went with them. The mother was lying on a cot, covered with a white sheet. A few neighbors came into the home. I did not say a word to anyone. I just did not know exactly what happened. But, I went and laid my hands on that woman's face under the sheet, and as I started to pray the woman vibrated with such a force that she rolled off the bed and fell to the floor. Then she stood up on her feet. We were all amazed! Whether the woman had died an hour or two before I do not know; I am not sure, but, as the girls said, mama had died. They had walked about half a mile and had come to meet me.

These miracles of healing and deliverance were very prevalent. And because of that, we had a breakthrough in the Hindu community and among the Muslims when they saw the power of God. They could not deny what they had seen, and so we built many churches around the region because of these miracles—Amen!

Lord, let her not break up the furniture or anything

One Saturday night in June, rain fell all night. That Sunday morning we were supposed to go to church, but before I got out of bed I heard somebody calling at my gate. My wife was in the kitchen and her sister was with her. I was in bed with my little girl. So I told my wife, "Open the door." But she felt as though there was something evil, and she would not open the door. I said, "It sounds like a sister that has come to go to church with us. Open the door. Open the door!" As she opened the door this woman, an African woman of about 190 pounds, her hair loose and wild, flew at her to grab her.

My wife ran into the bedroom. My sister-in-law leaped over my wife, over my little girl and me, and hit the wall; then she fell back on the bed. Oh, how that woman carried on! I closed the door, and said, "Lord, let her not break up the furniture or anything." Then I knelt down and I prayed in tongues for about ten minutes. As I was praying in tongues, I could hear this woman carrying on, speaking a language. I told my wife that I was going to go out, and she should close the door behind me.

My wife said, "No, please do not go. That woman will kill you."

I said, "No, it will be all right."

So I opened the door and she closed it behind me. I saw the woman. She looked as though she wanted to leap on me. Sitting on the edge of the chair, her eyes red like fire, ready to leap on me. An anointing just came on me as though I were suspended in the air. I rushed over to her and I touched her in the name of Jesus Christ. She fell and prostrated herself on the floor, wallowing.

After a while I helped her to her feet, and I led her out onto the veranda and sat there with her. I asked the demon in her what its name was. It answered me: "I am Simon Daimon, and I came from Tobago to kill this woman."

So, I said, "You demon of murder, I charge you in the name of Jesus—loose this woman, and go back from whence you came." The woman fell on the floor again. Nine times she got up, and then fell. Nine demons came out of her. [*See Luke 8:26–37.*] The last demon that came out of her hurt her. She grunted and groaned; then she got her release.

I said to her, "Do you know me?"

She said, "Yes, pastor."

I asked, "What happened to you?"

She said, "I left home; and the moment I stepped out into the road, it was like I was in a wilderness. I did not know where I was going. I was traveling through this wilderness, and I saw a light in this house. I came to it, but I did not know it was a house. I just kept calling."

God delivered that woman—set her free. The power of God *does* loose everyone—liberating all. Praise the name of Jesus!

The author encountered a demon-possessed girl in the psych ward of a hospital who, in response to prayer for her deliverance, babbled in a devilish "tongue." When the evil spirit was commanded to leave her, it threw the girl unconscious to the floor of her room. When she "came to," she was awed by the power of God, and was able to tell how she became possessed. She had been initiated by her grandmother into a sect of voodoo the previous year at her ancestral home in the Philippines. Unfortunately, she ultimately rejected Christ in favor of the supposed benefits of the "power" she had been granted by Satan! The knowledge that she would face eternity in hell did not seem to dissuade her from a life of sin.

A demon-possessed home

One day there was a report of a demon-possessed home in Siparia, a town in Trinidad in which one of our churches had been established. Stones fell. Iron fell in that house. The residents had to run out; they could not stay. In fact, people saw a man riding a bicycle up in the midst of the air inside the house. They called the local Roman Catholic priest to pray. While the priest was reading from his prayer book, a stone came from nowhere and knocked the book right out of his hand. The priest fled. Some policemen came in to investigate and check the damage that had been done to the house. While they were in the house, they saw this man riding this bicycle in midair and the iron hitting against the walls. They also fled from the place.

The Sunday morning after the baptismal service at our church in that town, I was in my car by the church. Some of the brethren who were with me had heard about the house and had gone to see for themselves. They came back and told me that the thing was real. There were a lot of spectators there. They knew that I was tired, but they offered to drive me there and bring me back if I would go to see the place. When we arrived I saw about 200 people standing in front of the house looking at it. I told them, "I will go in and pray." They did not favor that, but I told them that nothing would happen.

"And these signs shall follow them that believe..."

I went into the house, stood on the veranda, and read a passage of Scripture from the Gospel of Mark, chapter 16, verse 17: "And these signs shall follow them that believe; In my name shall they cast out devils; they shall speak with new tongues" (KJV). And I preached to the people. I told them about the resurrection of Jesus and the mighty power of God that He has given to His disciples. I said the power is evident today and is still available. After preaching I gave an altar call; everyone there gave their lives to Christ. Then I prayed. I charged the devil to loose that house and never torment it again. After the service was over, I told the residents that they could return and live in the house again and that nothing would happen to them.

The Mirror, one of our national papers, wanted to find out whom the man was who came to stop this thing, because it had gone on for a week. So I told them, "Tell the people it is Jesus of Nazareth, the Son of God that has put the devil to flight. He's alive!" Hallelujah!

God made the rain to obey our voice and even the creeping ants to hearken

The Lord called me to be a witness of His message of redemption throughout Trinidad. And so I was led, [at] one time, to take three of the brothers with me and go up to a Catholic monastery located on a mount on the Northern Range and to pray for the people there. I spoke to some young priests and was told that it is not permissible for them to speak to a non-Christian and that they did not think that they wanted us around. So we left and headed back.

Rather than return to Princes Town, we decided to stop and camp out in the fields nearby. The valley where we stopped was so cold we had to light a fire to keep warm. We hung our hammocks on some trees and decided to fast and pray for three days. We had no change of clothing and no food, and we drank water from a mountain stream. During the night we heard the rumbling of a rainstorm coming. With some very real concern, the brethren turned to me and said, "Look, we have no change of raiment, we are far away from home, and the place is cold. What shall we do?"

I stood on a rock, lifted my hands, and prayed that the Lord would cause the rain to cease. In a few minutes, it stopped. We all praised God and gave Him the glory for answering our prayer. But fifteen minutes later, the rain started with even greater intensity than before. You could hear the roaring sound of the rain in the forest. Again the brethren called my attention to the problem.

I said, "We need to pray." So I stood on the rock again,

lifted my hands, and, in the name of Jesus, commanded the rain to turn away. And that is precisely what happened.

On the second day of the fast, we were suddenly plagued with thousands upon thousands of soldier ants. The brethren came to me again and said, "Look, we cannot stand this. We need to get out of this place."

Immediately, the Lord put into my heart the need to command these ants to leave. I marched around, circling the area where we were staying, and commanded the ants to come no closer than the edge of our camp. And believe me, that is exactly what happened. Not another ant showed up until we were ready to leave. God made the rain to obey our voice and even the creeping ants to hearken. So we give God praise and glory and honor, for truly He is the God of the heavens and the earth, and the sea and all that's in it. His love and His power are without limit.

What Peter has just described may seem almost preposterous, even to Spirit-filled Christians; however, such things have been reported throughout the world and on a rather regular basis. The author has experienced, first hand, a number of such divine interventions. Remember, God will honor those who honor him.

The author has experienced the hospitality of the Hosein home on a number of occasions and during visits of up to a week at a time during the research work for this piece. It is a haven of rest for anyone who visits, and its doors are always open to their huge circle of friends and family. Peter's wife, Esther, models a life of faithfulness, wisdom, and generosity to the many Christian women she interacts with on a daily basis. I saw evidence of strong marriages in the local church. The following, final account may help the reader to understand one factor involved in the establishment of the Hosein home as a sanctuary for the lost and lonely.

...I took a page from the Bible

At the time I was building this house, here in Indian Walk, I took a page from the Bible—Genesis, chapter 28, which reports on Jacob's encounter with the Lord.

> When Jacob awoke from his sleep, he thought, "Surely the LORD is in this place, and I was not aware of it." He was afraid and said, "How awesome is this place! This is none other than the house of God; this is the gate of heaven." Early the next morning Jacob took the stone he had placed under his head and set it up as a pillar and poured oil on top of it. He called that place Bethel [house of God].
>
> —GENESIS 28:16–19

I put it in the front pillar of the house and I poured oil upon it and a piece of rock, and I told the Lord that this house was dedicated to the Lord for His honor and His glory. [I told Him] that the gate in front of this house should never be closed, night or day, but it should be left open that Your children passing by as pilgrims would turn in and find rest and quietness in this home. It seems to me that God heard that prayer and I can testify to the fact that ministers from all over this world have passed by and have found rest in this home. I feel so very honored that the Lord has heard my prayer and caused me to be a little instrument of blessing to the body of Christ.

This ends the testimony of Rev. Peter Hakim Hosein.

Chapter 9
REFLECTIONS OF A "PK"

On July 4, 2000, Joshua Hosein, Peter's son, at that time general secretary of the Foursquare Church in Trinidad, met with me in the United States to discuss what he believes is the vision God has given him for the twenty-first century expansion of the Foursquare in the south eastern region of the Caribbean.

During our time together I asked this dedicated young man to give his personal reflections on growing up in the household of a true servant of God. This chapter is Joshua's observations and impressions.

JOSHUA HOSEIN SPEAKS

Church was an absolute priority and an awesome celebration

As far back as I can remember, going to church was an absolute priority and an awesome celebration. How could I forget the time when my father suddenly interrupted his Sunday morning sermon and strode, with holy authority, into the midst of my brother and me as we thoughtlessly disturbed the service? Following a laying on of his hands at the seat of our rebellion, he returned to the pulpit and completed his message with what I remember to be an even greater anointing. We were truly raised in church. I will ever acknowledge with deep gratitude his determination to see that each of his children becomes "someone" in the Lord.

My father was a man committed to prayer and fasting. I still recall the time I pushed open the door to his room during one of his seasons of intense prayer—I was about four or five at the time. As I walked in he was speaking in tongues. I reached up toward him and he drew me up into his arms continuing to "pray in the Holy Ghost." Suddenly his prayers were transformed into holy laughter. At the time I couldn't understand how someone could mix laughing with praying. I started to laugh, too, because I thought it was like a joke. But now, having come of age and having walked in the joy of God's holy presence myself, I realize that what he was experiencing then was the "oil of gladness" spoken of by the prophet Isaiah (61:3, NAS). The holy laughter that came upon him was actually the response of the Holy Spirit to a father's love for his son; it just broke out through my own *abba's* (Aramaic for "father") spirit. The event is still vivid in my mind, as though it happened yesterday, and has affected my own ministry as well. I have seen many people break forth with this holy laughter as their spirit begins to experience the realization of the sin cleansing liberty of the cross of Christ.

> For an in-depth discussion of this particular gift of the Spirit, please refer to 1 Corinthians 12 and 14. Please study chapter 14 very carefully in its entirety.

My dad would take many trips across the seas. During one of his trips to the United States in the early 1970s he was offered a church, along with a house, car, and salary, and all moving expenses including airline tickets for the whole family. However, because of his love and burden for the people of Trinidad and Tobago and the Caribbean islands, he was not moved by the generous offer that would provide not only the opportunity to preach the gospel in the United States, but luxurious living for his family. He denied himself that he would remain in the center of God's will.

I have been tempted, quite recently, to come to the United States with my family and enjoy the quality of life there (luxurious when compared with much of the Caribbean). Of course I would preach the gospel on the side. However, as I spent time in prayer and looked back on the self-less obedience of my own father, I found myself prepared to listen as a fellow minister spoke "words of wisdom" into my spirit. I rethought my plans and decided to refuse the pleasures of this world for a season (see Hebrews 11:25) and to dwell with the people for whom God has burdened my heart. It seems that the mantle of preaching to the lost on these islands, a mantle carried so effectively by my father, has been transferred to me. I want to be wherever the Lord wants me to be.

I really feel the call; I feel it afresh. I sense an anointing, the equipping of the Holy Ghost to be in Trinidad and Tobago at this time, and to be in the midst of what God is about to do. If there is one thing that I have learned from my dad, it is this: we only pass this way once, and only that which is done for Christ will last! I want to see fruit that will remain. The impact that my dad has had on my life is really beginning to bear fruit—my decision to surrender fully to God's will has been accompanied with a simultaneous sense of His presence and power.

...an angel in the car?

When I was about eleven years old, I would do just about anything for the opportunity to drive my father's car; I would wash the car just to get to drive it from the garage out into the driveway. When I was finished, I would then drive it back into the garage. To wash the car meant to drive the car. And, once the car was clean, it seemed all right to drive it back and forth in the garage.

One afternoon I had this burning desire to drive the car. So, I backed the car out, washed it, and then accidentally locked the keys in the car. It was dusk— quite dark. I tried to open the door, but without success. Suddenly I began to think about the wrath of God coming on me through my father; he had an appointment to preach in a distant village. He had been fasting and praying that afternoon and seeking the Lord about what to share with those people. Knowing my father, you would clearly understand the excitement in his heart and the urgency he felt about reaching that village in time for the service.

Well, I kept trying to find a way to get into the car, but to no avail. Finally, my dad came downstairs, all dressed, Bible in hand, ready to go to his meeting. When he reached for the door to open it, he found it locked. He asked me for the keys. I said, "Well, I'm sorry. I accidentally locked the keys in the car." He said, "Oh, no!" He walked around the car puzzled, seemingly torn between dismay and anticipation. Hmm…what did the Lord have in mind; why has He allowed this? I myself wanted to know if I was going to live through the experience. Suddenly I didn't have a taste for driving any more.

My father told me to hold the Bible. He went on one of the sides of the front door and he started to pray. Well, I really thought he was beginning to "lose it." But he began to pray in earnest; and as he did, the lock button on one door began to rise miraculously, as though an invisible hand was pulling it up. Then he said, "Come, come, come and see this! Look, look! It's rising, it's rising…it's rising!"

And I came and looked but could not believe what I was seeing. I saw the button rising. It rose to the point where the door could be opened. My dad casually opened the door, took his Bible, and went off just as though everything was normal...usual! It was a dramatic turning point in my life. I just couldn't believe the miraculous intervention of God's hand there. Not only had God opened the door, He had saved my skin. I'll have you to know I got my license soon after that.

Was there an angel in the car?

She simply reached out and touched him

One time my father was preaching revival meetings at the church in the village of Gasparillo. A woman, who had suffered for years with an ulceration of the foot due to a circulatory problem, attended the services. She had been to all the physicians and hospitals that she knew of. She tried going to the witch doctors; she tried herbal medication. All her efforts were in vain. She was very discouraged. One night she began pleading with God, asking and trusting that she would be healed. Being a visitor to the church, she did not know my dad and felt that she was too poor and unworthy to approach him. So, after my dad was through preaching, she waited till he was passing by her in the aisle. She simply reached out and touched him on the hand. Instantly, she felt the power of God. She later testified that when she went home the sores immediately began to dry up. Great scabs began to form all over the sole of her foot. She knew she had experienced the healing power of the Lord Jesus.

Jesus said, "Anyone who has faith in me will do what I have been doing. He will do even greater things than

these, because I am going to the Father" (John 14:12).
I am reminded of the woman with the issue of blood
who touched the hem of Jesus' garments and was
immediately healed (Luke 8:43–48). Hallelujah!

...a cow by the name of Bundy

My father was not just a hard worker; he was also a
man of the Word and of prayer. People would call him the
"man and his book," because everywhere he went, he went
with his Bible in hand. And he would pray and preach. I
remember that up in the hills, behind the first church he
founded, he had a cow by the name of Bundy. He would go
and pray alongside Bundy. One day he was reading in the
Bible that all the cattle on all the hills belong to the Lord
(Ps. 50:10). When he read that, he said to the cow, "Bundy,
you belong to Jesus." He told me that when he said that,
Bundy bowed her head (in reverence?). My father was bold
and fearless in his witness for Christ, and in his proclamation of the name of Jesus. His faith is such that he believed
that Jesus Christ would back him up in everything he did
and said.

Peter marries Esther

Wilson Ramai of Ben Lomond Village, the man that gave
my dad the car, arrived in Trinidad in 1914 at the age of ten
with his parents who came by ship from India as indentured laborers/servants.[1]

Soon after meeting my father, he began to accompany
him as he went around preaching the gospel. Wilson Ramai
and his wife, Nita, had fourteen children—three boys and
eleven—one of whom was Esther. These girls would travel
and sing at crusades with my father and their dad, who by
now was also a preacher.

After they had sung one night, my dad asked one of the

girls, Esther, the pertinent question, "Would you marry me?" She thought it was a joke, but from the seriousness of his face and the anointing that seemed to be on his words, she responded with, "Yes, I will marry you." They were married on July 24, 1955 (my dad's birthday), and plans were made to go to Mayaro, a resort area, where they would spend their honeymoon.

Dad was given money for the trip, but used most of it to buy a PA system for the ministry. With the remainder he bought a large fish; he told mom she could have the fish because he was going to pray and fast. This was typical of him. Fasting and praying on his honeymoon! May God give us the strength He gave to him! He used the PA system to preach the gospel everywhere.

Out of this marriage four children were born: Sharon, Marilyn, Joshua, and Peter. The naming of each of the children was significant and dramatic. Dad was praying the night before I was born, and the Lord told him in a vision to call me Joshua—not for Joshua the successor of Moses but Joshua the high priest in the Book of Zechariah. The Lord told him to call me Joshua for I would "build the house of the Lord." When he heard that I was born and a boy, he said, "Let his name be called Joshua, for he shall build the house of the Lord."

It's interesting to note that after all these years, here I am actually fulfilling that prophetic word. I am building the house of the Lord, not only spiritually but physical structures as well. I have been spending a great deal of time lately rebuilding the churches that my dad first built. We are seeing considerable membership growth and the buildings are too small to contain the congregations. Some of the new buildings are from about thirty to forty feet wide by up to a hundred feet in length. It is amazing how God continues to supply the materials needed to make room for expansion. The Lord is also using me to build larger congregations through the stabilizing of leadership and through spiritual growth.

In 1980 my dad was preaching in a village called New Grant. As he was preaching he felt the call of God to go into the village of Hindustan, so named because of the dominance of the Hindu religion in that area. It was a distinct call to preach the gospel in that community. I had just started out in the ministry, and my sisters were involved as well in the ministry. We had formed a singing group named The Inspiration Singers. Dad preached; we the led worship.

As with most country areas of Trinidad, the houses in Hindustan were built up on timber or concrete stilts, the area below the house providing a perfect shelter from the weather. It was under such a house that we were given permission to meet.

This meeting went on for forty-five nights. There was a lot of rain and cold nights. It went through the Carnival season. Carnival is a cultural thing that is hosted once a year. It's a big celebration in Trinidad. It is essentially the same as Mardi Gras in the United States. There is a lot of reveling, a lot of drunkenness, and a lot of immorality in our island around this time; so it's dangerous to be having a crusade of this nature out in the open. Traveling was precarious because of the drunkenness on the road and the gross immorality. However, the Lord beckoned us to continue on with the meetings so we kept on going.

Out of this crusade came thirty-five people who were baptized (water baptized), filled with the Holy Spirit, and going on to serve the Lord. We also have a few leaders who came out of the crusade who are presently involved in pastoral ministry and in other gifted positions in the body of Christ.

Another church we started was built in an unusual place—a mud volcano known as the Devil's Woodyard. Its name has been attributed to the apparent evidence of fearful spiritist or other occult behavior or patterns witnessed by a number of people in the area. Over the years we have seen many Hindus and Muslims come to know the Lord as their Savior through that particular work.

This ends the testimony of Joshua Hosein.

Chapter 10
THE STONES SPEAK OUT
What Others Say about This Servant of God

The information in this chapter has been incorporated into this volume for two distinct reasons: (1) it is more evidence supporting the authenticity and integrity of the Rev. Peter Hosein, and (2) it offers the reader additional anecdotal evidence of the continued direct work of the Holy Spirit in the twentieth and twenty-first century ministry.

PART 1: PETER'S WIFE

Is a man real? Ask his wife; she will know better than anyone whether or not his life is authentic or just a stage play. The following accounts of incidents in Peter's life are told by Mrs. Esther Hosein:

"The Lord will keep you from all harm—he will watch over your life" (Psalm 121:7)

One night while my husband and one of our missionaries, Brother B from Grenada, were in Siparia to conduct some evangelistic meetings, I decided to go to bed early. I lit one of those mosquito coils and hung it over the bed as I often did. Then I dozed off. Somehow the coil fell and ended up under the buffalo pillow—a sort of stuffed cotton pillow—I was laying my head on. The pillow ignited and apparently smoldered for quite some time. Meanwhile, down in Siparia, the Holy Spirit told my husband to close the service immediately and go right home. He obeyed. As he arrived, he saw that the house was filled with smoke.

As he entered the room, the pillow just burst into flames—and my head was still on it! Peter got there just in time. That man used to pray and fast! He lived in tune with the Spirit.

When my son, Peter, was about eight months old, he contracted a form of dysentery. One month before this my husband's sister's child died from this very same sickness. On the Sunday of that particular week, my husband left us at home and went to the Cumuto church. He stayed over at his brother's home after church until the evening service. Suddenly I saw little Peter's eyes turn up. His body lay lifeless. I called a neighbor to "get a bicycle and ride down to the church to get Brother Hosein." Peter came back with his car and prayed for our son; and then [he] went back [to the church]. Healing was almost instantaneous!

...if I could just touch him I would be healed

One night I was feeling as though I was dying. I got very weak; I felt as though I was sinking inside. So, since Peter (my husband) was sleeping, I felt that if I could just touch him I would be healed. I touched him on his body and felt completely restored, instantly. I told him about it in the morning.

> *This event brings to mind the biblical accounts of Matthew 9:20, Mark 5:25, and Luke 8:43, which report on a very significant event in the ministry of Jesus Christ during His time on earth. A woman that had been chronically ill for a period of twelve years reached out in an act of faith and touched Jesus as He was engulfed by a huge crowd of people. She was instantly healed. Jesus suddenly stopped what He was doing and remarked that someone had touched Him.*

His disciples very intelligently informed Jesus that certainly He had been touched; He was in the middle of a huge crowd. Jesus then set them straight: He actually felt a vitalizing power exit His body and bring healing to someone in need. The woman then identified herself.

...he saw a light in the church

My husband's brother s twelve-year-old daughter suddenly became dumb and crippled. She could hear but could not speak or walk. When they took her to the doctor, he said the girl was just playing tricks. She remained like this for about three months. I am a witness of this. She could laugh but not walk or talk. She needed assistance to get to the bathroom. She could move her hands but not her legs. My husband decided with others in the church to fast and pray. (During those three months he was fasting and praying for her.)

The day she got healed he saw a light in the church. He alone saw this bright light. When he saw the bright light he went and prayed for her and she was immediately healed. She is now married, has two beautiful children and lives in Canada.

This ends the testimony of Esther Hosein.

PART 2: BROTHER HILTON DONOVAN

The first pastor of the church at Basse Terre-Moruga, southern Trinidad, was Brother Hilton Donovan, the man Peter Hosein often referred to as "Don." Hilton Donovan served as Peter Hosein's right-hand man during the early 1960s, a time when Peter's church planting ministry began to reach out, successfully, beyond Trinidad. Again, we see the evidence and the benefit of Peter's obedience to the strategy laid out by the Word of God—to go and make disciples of men. Peter did not recruit from a seminary; he raised up ministers of the gospel along with the establishment of new churches. Pastor Donovan was first converted (born again) at a house meeting conducted by Peter on a Sunday night in August 1959 in St. Madeleine, Trinidad.

During the research phase of this account, the author and his wife had the privilege of spending a weekend with Brother Donovan and his lovely wife, Laurie, at their home in Louisville, Kentucky, USA. We were graced with wonderful Caribbean food, one of God's blessings that flow from that part of the world. My purpose was to record the thoughts of one who worked on a day-to-day basis with Peter in the battle to win souls for Christ.

The following is Hilton Donovan's testimony and his observations of the ministry of Peter Hosein.

Pastor Donovan's observations

A series of prayer meetings were being held in my hometown. A friend of mine and I decided to attend. For no apparent reason I found myself crying and sobbing—my heart was being broken. There was an overwhelming awareness of the presence of God in that prayer meeting. I began crying out to the Lord for mercy and compassion. A young minister got up and read a few scriptures from the Bible and talked about the love of Jesus. Then he asked if anyone wanted to receive Christ as their personal and indwelling Savior. I quickly got up and raised my hands and invited Jesus to come in. From that time on I began serving the Lord.

Very soon after my conversion, Rev. Hosein laid his hands on me and others during a Holy Ghost rally, as they were called in those days. I was immediately filled with the Holy Spirit and spoke in tongues. Soon after that I was baptized in water. It was at that time that I felt a call to preach the gospel, a calling that was coupled with a strong love for Jesus Christ and the souls of men. Rev. Hosein directed me into a course of studies: an advanced Bible course and studies in personal evangelism. After that we teamed up to preach the gospel. I would begin the services: opening in prayer, leading the singing, and reading the scriptures— whatever was necessary to prepare the congregation for the preaching of the Word by Peter Hosein

Since I had grown up in the Anglican church, my mother was very displeased that I was now a "born again" Christian. We were Anglicans, and she was an Anglican lady! She did not like the idea of my leaving the church to go into the "small church," as she termed it. My brother also was very displeased with me joining this "new religion." I began to experience severe persecution from my family. I was being encouraged to abandon my new faith…and the Lord. However, following considerable prayer, the Lord gave me strength and the courage to leave home. Subsequently, the Holy Spirit spoke to my spirit and encouraged me to arise and go to the home of the Rev. Hosein and stay with him and his family for a time. I told him what I felt, what the Lord had said to me, and explained the situation. He gladly took me in. I stayed with the Hoseins a number of years; he became my spiritual covering. My association with him was something else! I lived in and out of his house for over four years—until I was married.

During that time I was privileged to see his family grow— his children: Sharon, Elvis [Joshua], Marilyn, and Peter.

They were all young kids then. Many a time we returned from evening crusades and meetings at a late hour. I often carried them up into the house and into bed, careful not to awaken them.

Living with that family, I learned a lot. I learned especially in the area of intercessory prayer. We preached the gospel throughout the length and breadth of south Trinidad with great results. One of the things that made us so very successful in these crusades and meetings was the hours of prayer spent before every event. We prayed and prayed and prayed during the day, awaiting God's anointing, and then preached at night. Often the preaching was coupled with the actual construction of a new church building in the vicinity of our crusade. We spent the days simultaneously praying, fasting, and building churches. Revival was always there; it was in the air! It was soon after this that I decided to get married.

Many times he would agonize in prayer, waiting to "pray through"

The Rev. Peter Hosein was a very prayerful man. Honestly, my own life of prayer was the result of the inspiration I received from him. Many times he would agonize in prayer, waiting to "pray through," that the anointing for that evening's meeting was on him and that they could expect fruit. Many times, whether through a prophetic word or through a deep inner conviction, he would hear from God and would express to us what would happen that night. I know that the practice of waiting on God so many, many times in prayer was the very reason for the success of these crusades. In fact the old International Pentecostal Assembly (IPA) was founded on prayer and fasting.

> *"Praying through" is a traditional expression meaning to await the inner conviction that the prayers have been heard. This practice is confirmed by 1 John 5:14–15: "This is the confidence we have in approaching God: that if we ask anything according to his will, he hears us. And if we know that he hears us—whatever we ask—we know that we have what we asked of him."*

...a burden to expand his work

As soon as a base of churches had been established throughout the length and breadth of Trinidad, Peter began to experience a burden to expand his work to Grenada, St. Vincent, and the other islands. At this time I was the pastor of the Basse Terre-Moruga, church. In fact I was the first one to be ordained as pastor of that church. And it was then I felt the need to be married and have a life companion who would be a suitable partner in the ministry. I can clearly remember that a couple of us young guys in the church prayed continually and very fervently for a "help meet"— a good wife (Gen. 2:18, KJV). It wasn't long before God answered all our prayers.

Again the Rev. Peter Hakim Hosein became an instrument of blessing in my life. One day he and I and Brother B, another minister, were traveling in a car. Rev. Hosein had a letter with him from a Miss Laurie Jack of Grenada, a member of one of the families that attended a new church he had planted there in Westerhall about two years before. [*The Westerhall church in Grenada was planted in 1960 by Peter Hosein.*] Both Peter and Brother B exclaimed that this would be the perfect wife for me.

> *As Hilton continued in his prayers from this point on, he began to get visions of a woman that he was sure was Laurie Jack. She just appeared to him wearing*

white clothes and had a bouquet in her hands. The visions were so clear, that when he first met his bride-to-be in person on his first trip to Grenada, he was amazed that every feature of the woman was identical to that portrayed in the vision. He sent a letter to Miss Laurie Jack in November of 1962 telling her that he loved her based on the Spirit's vision. He had not actually seen her or her picture. Laurie hesitated until she had seen a picture of him, then: "I fell in love with him because of how nice and kind he was. I wanted a husband that was stronger in the Lord than me." Hilton was sent to Grenada the following month at which time he and Laurie were engaged. He returned in April to be married and to pastor the church there, an assignment he carried out till his calling to St. Vincent with Peter Hosein in 1964.

...the time had come to go to go St. Vincent

This account was reported earlier by Peter Hosein. Such retelling of anecdotal material mirrors similar parallels in the Bible itself. Slight variances, where they occur, actually reinforce the authenticity of an event. No two people stand on the same piece of ground while viewing an action; thus, the variance in view.

After a successful series of meetings in Grenada, and having completed the building of churches there, he [Peter] told me that he felt a call from God that the time had come to go to St. Vincent, a call to carry the message of salvation and deliverance to the folks there. He had mentioned this calling many times previously, but there always seemed to be an obstacle set by the Spirit. Then came the time when he really got the breakthrough. He called the church there together and said, "Pastor Don and I will be going to St. Vincent to carry the gospel of deliverance there."

(He had never been there before. About two or three years went by before the trip to St. Vincent first happened. He kept on praying for St. Vincent that the day would come when he would be able to go there. The day came, and he decided to take me with him.)

We didn't know anyone there, except that my father-in-law, Mr. Jack, knew a man, a Mr. T, who grew up with him in the Edinburgh area of St. Vincent. My father-in-law said to look up this Mr. T and tell him that Mr. Jack asks that he would help them. We left in March 1964 on an interisland passenger boat, the *Federal Palm*, arriving in St. Vincent the next day. Having found Mr. T, we were then led to Richland Park, near Mesopotamia Valley north of Kingston, the capital. My wife's grandparents had come from this area.

A wonderful old man, "Pa John," invited us to "pitch our tent" there, so to speak. And we did. The next day we set up the PA system and started by playing records of the Chuck Wagon Gang. We had the first meeting the night after we got there. We preached for a week, ending on a Saturday night. By the end of the week the attendance had grown to about 4,000. People came from the villages of Richland Park and Mesopotamia, and buses brought people from Kingstown. We did no advertising, distributed no leaflets, and made no radio announcements. Nothing! The anointing was so heavy that people just came. They were blessed and satisfied because we prayed for the sick. The word just spread. It was very, very amazing. That crusade in St. Vincent changed my life regarding missions. St. Vincent was my maiden journey in evangelism. Grenada was a family church, a sister church to those in Trinidad, and I found my wife there. But through that experience on St. Vincent, the importance of missions became very clear to me. It also became an integral part of Peter Hosein's ministry at that time.

We eventually built a church in St. Vincent. We built a nice church over there on land that was leased to us free. Later a piece of land was obtained permanently at another spot. We made two trips back to St. Vincent after that crusade. It was on the third trip that we actually started to build the church. Peter left me there as pastor, and Laurie and I stayed there for about a year and a half.

During that initial one-week crusade, the devilish opposition was fierce and it was mostly of a religious nature. A rather well-known Christian sect was the primary source. In the middle of the week, Rev. Hosein announced that on Friday everyone should bring their Bibles, some paper, and a pen because he would be telling them about the seven dispensations of God. His message was the most powerful of the entire week! He began by teaching on the Dispensation of Innocence in the Garden of Eden and continued on through the Dispensation of Grace. "For the law was given through Moses; grace and truth came through Jesus Christ." (John 1:17).

This caused a great stir in the village; that particular sect had a grip on the people, keeping them bound under the now outdated dispensation of Law. They were very offended and very displeased with the message. They called us false prophets. There was a great uproar. Some believed and some doubted. Some people said that "these people came to make confusion here." Peter was called a false prophet, and they wanted to beat him. Referring to Peter, they said, "We are going to beat him tonight." However, a taxi driver, a distant cousin of my wife through her grandparents, knew all the people in that area. And when they were getting ready to beat [Peter], [the taxi driver] spoke out to the crowd and said, "If you touch these two men there will be [an ethnic] riot. That caused the people to back off. He was a very popular guy in the area, and a roughneck too.

On the final night they gave us a fine send off. Everyone testified; "Thank God for sending these men to us from Trinidad and Grenada, for bringing light to us." When my wife and I went to live there a year afterward, they were still singing the same songs—"When Your Anchor Holds" and other rousing camp meeting songs. The kids used to sing them on their way to school. During that first revival, Peter Hosein was invited to preach at a prep school in Kingstown, the capital. Years later during a return visit to St. Vincent, a young man came up to him. He told Peter that he had gotten saved during his address at the school; now he was the attorney general for St. Vincent.

During that crusade, Peter had a dream one night. In the dream, a man came to him with a scroll, a document that was soaked in blood. The man was Jesus. When he opened the document he saw it was the gospel, the Word of God in the form of a deed. Peter told the congregation that night what he had dreamt. The interpretation of the dream was this: God had given Peter the power and authority to establish a permanent work there and to build a church. (The congregation had been asking him all week, "Are you going to stay here and start a work?" This was the answer they had been looking for, an answer ordained by the Lord Himself.) The whole congregation went immediately into a great time of worship. Eventually, one other work was started in St. Vincent, somewhere near Kingstown.

An interesting sidelight is the response of Peter's own IPA pastors during a ministry fellowship meeting held immediately following the St. Vincent crusade. They doubted the number of 4,000 responders. [*What else is new?*]

During one of the preparatory prayer times prior to a crusade meeting, Peter got up suddenly and said, "Don, I just felt a word of assurance from God. Whenever you go into a village, long before you appear before the people, you must first bind the strongman in that area and release the people. Then you go out to the meeting at night and use the same phrase to declare deliverance during the meeting as a formality. Nevertheless, doing this while you are in your prayer time on your knees in advance is what is crucial." It was very remarkable. He received that during prayer. The sequence was that in prayer long before the meetings we would (1) bind the strongman, (2) release, or loose, the people, and then (3) at the meeting declare the deliverance to the people. In our day it worked wonders. This became the rule for all subsequent crusade work.

This ends the testimony and reflections of Hilton Donovan.

PART 3: PHILLIP ALI

Phillip Ali, now living in North America, is a first cousin of Peter Hosein (their fathers were brothers), and was a close associate of Peter's during the early years of his ministry's expansion (probably from 1949 through 1966) . Phillip recalled that Peter was converted just by reading the Gospel of John. His typical early approach to sharing his newfound faith was "to gather up a couple of people—on a street corner or under the veranda of shops. The owners would often provide the light. Peter preached with power and fervor. Many made decisions to follow Jesus; he was

*very successful among the Muslims and the Hindus,"
who primarily populated the area. "Entire families
became saved. The earliest church was the Cumuto
church, and that church is still flourishing to this date."*

*The following are excerpts from the author's inter-
view with Phillip Ali during the summer of 2005.*

Peter preached with power and fervor

Before the Cumuto church was built, Peter's brother
Tazmool's home there was the center of the early church. At
that time Peter operated a rum shop (liquor store) in Indian
Walk, the village where he lived. When Peter got a revelation from God that this was wrong, he quit that business.
His oldest brother then gave up the license to sell liquor and
they closed the shop.

Some of the places where Peter blazed a trail and set up
churches were: Cumuto Road, Morne Diablo, Clark Rochard,
Monkey Town, New Grant, Rio Claro, Barrackpore, Borde
Narve, Gasparillo, Saint Clements, Cedar Hill, San Fernando
(Coffee Street), and the islands of Tobago, Grenada, and St.
Vincent. I can vouch for all of this.

In one particular area we were called out to pray for
the sick and pray for people who were possessed by the
devil. People would be kicking and screaming and spitting on you. As soon as Peter walked into whatever room
we were ministering in, he began to speak and to pray and
to pray in tongues. It appeared that the demons began to
act up a little more. Then, in one instance I can testify to,
as he laid his hands on a particular individual, the man
began to shake like a leaf. Afterwards, once the evil spirit
had left him, he became as calm as a baby. It was such an
amazing thing!

I recall one great revival that took place in Morne Diablo
(pronounced "mornjablo"), about fifteen to twenty miles

from Cumuto in the Penal area. Here is how it happened: apparently, one person heard Hakim (Peter) preaching. He invited him to the area and opened his home for him to preach. He invited his friends and neighbors and pitched a tent—really a covering to shade themselves from weather. That revival lasted about three weeks. Many people in that area got saved, healed, released from bondage to evil spirits, and confessed Jesus as Lord. I was part of that team; I was the song leader in the Cumuto church and served with him in the ministry. This was around 1952–1953.

Then I became a school teacher at Clark Road (Rochard), and it was here that another outpouring took place. While teaching at that school, I came in contact with three Christians: a Sister S and two others. They had been praying that there would be a church started. I got Hakim (Peter) involved and we began to hold meetings at the school and at peoples' homes. Eventually, we built a church there, which is also still flourishing. This was a Hindu area.

> *The now famous Hebrides Revival, which took place in the islands off the west coast of Scotland, began as a direct result of two women, one a shut-in, praying intercession for the youth of their area. They had been grieved by the very worldly lifestyle becoming common just after World War II.*

You could not dispute the power

I was also involved in the establishment of a small church in Monkey Town. This was a Presbyterian area, also primarily populated by Hindus. We only had one car; on Sunday nights one of us would go to Clark Rochard by car, the other to Monkey Town on a bike.

People flocked to hear [Peter]. Something was drawing them. You could not dispute the power with which he spoke;

and he was not speaking with notes. He would simply take a text—he knew the Bible that well—and the message came to him. It was like a water tap that was turned on; when the message was finished, the tap was turned off.

There were many other areas—a great work was done in Gasparillo with many converted. A wonderful church was built there also, it is still prospering today. As a matter of fact, my wife and I got married in that church. I worked in a government school there for one week, and then was transferred to another school. In that one week I made a connection that opened the way for starting that work.

Then there was the Moruga area—a Spanish-speaking, highly Catholic area, which was also Hindu and Muslim. Peter made contact with one particular family in that area. They loved to hear him preach. They got saved. This is how it all starts. Their friends came out to the meetings. They got together and built a lovely church. Peter was not one who would stand back [and let others do the hard work]. He gave of his effort. He did framing, poured concrete, laid blocks; then at six o'clock he would get cleaned up and would have a meeting right there before going home. There is an outstanding church there today.

Hakim (Peter) was an excellent cricketer. In the early days of his ministry he would play on Sundays—after church he would go and play cricket. But an accident took place one day. He was hit in the eye with the ball [a cricket ball is even harder than a baseball]. He came home. He felt God had allowed this to happen to him to show him that it was not right for him to be playing cricket on the Lord's Day. And, do you know what? He was an excellent spin bowler, and a batsman who was in the lineup to become a famous cricketer, one who would represent the West Indies. This is fact! In their test matches, he was being groomed for one of those spots. And yet, he just dropped it right there. He was in his twenties at the time.

His home at the time was in Indian Walk. The area at the back of the shop where they worked was a haven for me. I practically lived there for a time. One day Peter and a group of fellows decided that the thing to do was to fast and pray. So, he, his brother Esau, and Bros. Ashman and James went up to a place called the Maracas Valley, a secluded area in the Northern Range out of the reach on anyone. One fellow couldn't handle the fast after three days and came back. The other guys (I don't know how many days they each fasted, but I can testify that Peter fasted for twenty-one days) fasted and prayed, taking only water.

There was one brother (one of the early converts) who prayed and fasted for forty days and nights only on water. This I know to be a fact. Anyway, he entered the fast very sick. When he came out of it, he was completely rejuvenated physically. I don't understand all of it. I myself have fasted three and a half days. They say that your hunger disappears after the third day and returns on the sixth. On the ninth day it goes again and then you feel completely normal—just drinking water. Of course, prayer helps a lot. The heavy emphasis on fasting took place in the early part of his ministry—somewhere between 1954 and 1957.

> **Author's question to Phillip:** *"Do you recall any-thing significant happening as a result of this?"* The
> *following quote is his answer.*

Well, let me tell you—it would appear like the glory of God—when this guy gets up to preach, no one could stand the power of his words. If you've committed something wrong, you would get the feeling that he was pointing at you as he preached. You'd feel unclean! The presence of God was really evident. People came with their sicknesses and left healed. And something else: when he prayed for them, they'd be prostrate. No one was pushing them down. Perhaps the most important thing that was taking place was that people were getting saved. They were crying out— crying out because of their sins. It was real penitence. There were lots of tears and lots of crying and asking for pardon and forgiveness. Perhaps this was most evident because of his spending time in prayer and fasting and relying totally on God's Word and preaching as God revealed Himself.

His mother, who was my *chachi* (East Indian for "aunt"), was a wonderful lady. Hakim eventually had the opportunity to lead her to Jesus. When she was in her room dying, she was singing and praying and having a time of thanksgiving with glory and praise to God. Then, just like that, she passed away—in that atmosphere of glory and praise to God. She was a very kind person. I know; I spent a lot of time at her house. She cooked for us, cleaned us up, washed our clothes, and took care of us. I am indebted to that family.

> *Although Peter first experienced the empowering (referred to by some as the infilling) of the Holy Spirit, as initially given to the early church on the Day of Pentecost, at the age of eighteen, his emphasis in ministry up until this time had been the salvation of souls through the preaching of the cross. The time came, however, when the Lord apparently wanted Peter's team to bring the new believers to the next step in their discipleship: the Spirit empowered life and ministry as first taught by Jesus.*

...surrendered, Spirit-empowered life

As a result of Peter's surrendered, Spirit-empowered life, the church was growing leaps and bounds. His organization was also growing and becoming a little unwieldy. So we considered affiliating with another group, such as the New Testament Church of God (NTCOG), to administrate and oversee the work. One day, Peter took his team to one of their churches in Montrose. They were hosting a meeting led by an American evangelist. He began to talk to them about how they can be filled with the Holy Spirit and convinced them that the initial evidence of the infilling is speaking in tongues. So, at this meeting in Pointe-a-Pierre, these guys were really hungering and thirsting for the infilling of the Holy Spirit. As the missionary walked around and instructed them how they could receive the Holy Spirit, God was even *more* willing to give them the Spirit than they were willing to receive Him. And as he prayed for them, somehow they were able to release—how shall I put it?—God took over their vocal cords. They began to speak in another language. It was like bedlam [sic]. Everyone was speaking in a different language. They had an open air meeting that night and not knowing that "the spirits of the prophets are subject to the prophets" (1 Cor. 14:32, KJV), when they got up to speak all they could do was just spew out messages in different languages. Some of them had been slain in the Spirit for three or four hours—some laughing—just praising God in a different (or unknown) tongue.

A similar occurrence took place while the Jews were in the wilderness following their time of captivity in Egypt. God commanded Moses to call the seventy elders to the tent of meeting where He would take of the Spirit that He had put on Moses and put the Spirit on the elders of Israel so that they would be empowered to share in the work assigned by the Lord to Moses. Some of the elders happened to be out in the camp among the people at the time for God's outpouring on them. Those particular men began to prophesy out in the camp areas and the people thought something unusual was going on. Joshua criticized them to Moses, but Moses rebuked him, "I wish that all the LORD'*s people were prophets and that the* LORD *would put his Spirit on them!" (Num. 11:29; see verses 16–30). A similar phenomenon took place at the time when Samuel anointed Saul to become Israel's first king.*

...began to share...the baptism of the Holy Spirit

There had been many revivals before this time, but it was at this time that Peter's group began to come under the covering of the NTCOG. It was at the minister's meeting with the NTCOG that [the previously referred to missionary] spoke, and all of Peter's leaders were filled, including evangelist Sam Mathura, a well-known healing evangelist in the area. It was after this that Peter and his group returned to their mission field and began to share this doctrine of the baptism of the Holy Spirit with the initial evidence of speaking in other tongues to their congregations.

Another of Peter's early disciples and ministers was Brother Hilton Donovan who lived at the time in St. Clements. We were holding meetings in the St. Clements area, and Brother Donovan got saved at one of them. [It was there that] I met my wife. I was the one carrying on the service there one night, and during the service I spotted this girl. Without much form or ceremony, I asked this girl to marry me. She thought I was nuts. I courted her for four years after that and eventually we did get married. We have now been married for forty-four years.

Donovan learned quickly. He was able to give a testimony in the open. He was able to take a scripture and build a little sermon around it. There was one important thing about Hakim, and people liked this so much: the reason why there were so many young preachers in his group is that he gave them opportunity. He was a discipler. Although he planned to preach the main sermon, he would say, "Hey, Phillip, you give a short message or give a short testimony," or "Donovan, hey, you lead the singing tonight; give a little sermon." And because of these experiences most of these guys learned how to say a few scriptures, learned how to give a testimony and not be shy! And from that there were a lot of young little preachers [that he developed.]

Then we would be given a post. "You're in charge of that post; you're in charge of this post." We made mistakes, but you know what? We had a good heart for it. People saw our sincerity and our desire to preach the Word of God. We used our own time and money—our own effort. The people recognized that we were not in this to be popular or anything like that; we just wanted to be of service.

But, Donovan was a budding preacher in his early days. So from there he was sent by the NTCG to Grenada. He lived there quite a while. He met and married his wife there.

Brother Donovan became the initial pastor for the church at Basse Terre-Moruga.

Then there was the time when we as a group would meet in a tunnel in a remote area on Saturday nights. There was Hakim, Brother John, Brother Sam, and some other leaders. There was a lot of fasting that went on there. This was the secret of their success: Eating together in unity, uniting in prayer and praise, and then fasting and exercising that anointing that we could actually feel.

This ends the testimony and reflections of Phillip Ali.

Is it possible the church is missing this nowadays... this denial of the flesh and the total reliance on the Holy Spirit's power?

PART 4: DR. STEPHEN MOHAMMED

Dr. Stephen Mohammed is currently the pastor of the Balmain Worship Centre, New Testament Church of God, in Couva, Trinidad. Over the years he has held such important positions as seminary professor and national overseer of the New Testament Church of God in Trinidad and Tobago. The following is a condensation of the author's interview with Dr. Mohammed in January of 2004.

I first met Rev. Peter Hosein in the year 1953

I first met Rev. Peter Hosein in the year 1953; I was a young lad at the time. He came to Iere Village where our family lived and was preaching at a house meeting about two doors down from our home. I recall his preaching was very well received and large numbers were attracted to the meetings. A church was subsequently constructed nearby. Rev. Hosein came to the meetings on Tuesday nights by bicycle; his preaching style and manner of conducting a service were in stark contrast with that of the established Presbyterian Church located just opposite where Peter held his meetings. This caused quite a stew in the area. In fact, I think one can say with reasonable confidence and accuracy that Rev. Hosein would have been the first person to introduce Pentecostal evangelicalism into the community of Iere Village. There was the Spiritual Baptist Church there, and, of course, the Presbyterians are evangelicals; but as far as the emphasis on salvation and healing—the full gospel, so to speak—Rev. Hosein was certainly the first person to have introduced that kind of phenomenon to the community of Iere Village.

His preaching was such a success that the body he was associated with at the time, Christian General Assembly, constructed a church there next to where I lived. Services were held on Sundays and on Tuesday evenings. I started attending on Tuesday evenings. The first Tuesday night in October of 1953—I remember well that night—Rev. Hosein preached on Mark 1:17: "Come, follow Me, and I will make you fishers of men."

He gave an altar call. I am not sure I understood everything he said, he spoke very fast. I didn't understand all the Christian jargon. The terminology was foreign to me. I grew up as a Muslim, and he used such terms as "getting saved." That stuff was all somewhat alien; nevertheless, I remember very well the first Tuesday night in October 1953 when I just went to the altar and received Christ as my Savior and Lord. I was saved. A few months after that my sister, who still attends Peter Hosein's church at Cumuto, was also saved. She and I would often go to Princes Town and from there get a ride to the Cumuto church.

One Sunday morning, probably early in 1954, while Rev. Hosein was still at Iere Village pastoring, my sister and I were baptized by Rev. Hosein. That was my early encounter with this servant of God. That started a long relationship, and Rev. Hosein became very attached to our family. He became a personal mentor of mine.

Around July 1954, I began to feel an urge to preach the gospel. I had intended to be a criminal lawyer; somehow that was changed. God called me to the ministry. At that time I did not understand what all of that was. Now, looking back at the experience, I can describe what was happening to me in theological terms; but at that time it was "an urge." So, I went to Bible school. I left home. I left everything I was doing, and on the thirtieth of August, 1954, I went to Bible school at Pointe-a-Pierre. Rev. Hosein lectured at that Bible school. I still remember his lectures on spiritual gifts. In those days we were very zealous and had a strong passion to be used by God.

...the only vision that God truly honors and brings to fruition is that which seeks to glorify Him, not man

Then, one day during the class, Rev. Hosein made what I think was a crisis statement for my own life. He said, "I observed that you young men are very zealous and want to be used of God." Then he asked," Why do you want to be used of God...why?" He asked us to examine that issue. Was it that we might become prominent, or that God might be glorified? He then went on to explain—it still rings in my spirit—that the only vision that God truly honors and brings to fruition is that which seeks to glorify Him, not man. This divine principle has had a tremendous impact on my life. Now I am almost sixty-six years of age. This is 2004. Every time I stand up to minister the Word of God, I remember it. "Am I doing this for my glory or am I doing it for the glory of God?" It was a revolutionizing experience.

It is still vibrant to me. That was just one of the incidents in which this man had a powerful impact on my life.

Then, of course, both of us got married into the same family and that brought us even closer. Pastor Hosein got married to Esther, and I married Esther's younger sister Helen. Our common father-in law was also a minister, so we often traveled together to minister's meetings and conventions. And it was in those family gatherings, those times of fellowship, that Brother Hosein was able to influence us with his ministry. We started to look at him somewhat as a prophet of God. At least in my mind I saw him as having a heavy prophetic anointing. Later on, as I further explored the subject of spiritual gifts, I was convinced that the word of wisdom (1 Cor. 12:8, KJV) operated in his life. In fact, the operation, or manifestation, of that particular gift in his life impacted me so powerfully, that I later made a detailed study of spiritual gifts. One of my major works was on spiritual gifts. So he influenced me in that respect as well.

I was then called to pastor a church. From there I went on to the University of the West Indies. From my subsequent position as principal of the Open Bible High School, I rose to the position of national overseer of the New Testament Church of God with the oversight of several churches. Again, I attribute all of this to that mighty man of God, a man used by God to bring me to the truth. So I would say: my whole life—everything I am—I owe to the Lord, of course; but I owe a great deal to this faithful instrument.

The decisions I make today on my job, the way I operate, my response to issues— these are all colored by the fact that Rev. Hosein has become a major point of reference. I look back to see how he responded to similar situations and carefully considered the wisdom of his decisions at the time.

God has blessed me in many, many ways, and I thank Him for that; but Rev. Hosein did play a large part in my life.

...through this instrument of total surrender to God, I was again brought to life

Then another time of crisis came into my life: I got very ill. It was 1967 or 1968 and I became very sick in those years. Rev. Hosein took my wife and me in and kept us for a long time. He and his wife personally ministered to us and nursed me back to health. I was almost dying. I had wasted away; and through this instrument of total surrender to God, I was again brought to life. So much of my present life I owe to him.

Looking back to the early days of my ministry with him (it was about 1955), I recall the time Rev. Hosein conducted a crusade in Lower Barrackpore. One of his nephews and I used to go early in the afternoon to invite people out to the meetings. It was held in a school yard. Hundreds of people attended that meeting that Rev. Hosein called a campaign— we would say "crusade," but his term was "campaign." We would go early and set up the microphones—the public address system, then go into the community and invite people to come to that night's meetings. We would also follow up with those who had given their lives to the Lord. Hundreds of people came to that crusade; it was very well attended. Large numbers of people were born again; in fact, a church was established as a result of that crusade.

...I saw light, a glow like that from a light bulb— there was radiance

The following experience was particularly noteworthy. One evening Rev. Hosein was ministering in the crusade. When I looked at him—it still puzzles me—I saw light, a glow like that from a light bulb—there was a radiance.

That night everybody around him fell down. As the people were encompassed by the radiance they just fell; then they started to pray. Many of those people became part of the church that he built in that community. That event still stands out in my mind.

There was also another very, very supernatural intervention of God in his life and ministry in that particular area. A number of us were with him. He went to pray for a demon-possessed person. I was frightened. He just went in and started casting out the demons and the demons started to name names. Rev. Hosein's response to these evil spirits became a point of reference for me when I observe the modern behavior of casting out demons. That demon (or at least one of them) was saying his name was Simon Daimon.

The word daimon is a term found in Greek literature referring to an upper echelon devilish spirit.

Rev. Hosein said to the demon, "I don't know if that's your name or that you are lying. You are a liar and I rebuke you." The possessed person was miraculously delivered that night and came to the crusade. I don't know what has become of her, but that was an outstanding, divine intervention.

For him to not even focus on the name of the demon or to recognize that a demon could be lying had to be divine revelation. We are talking about 1955, not the twenty-first century where we have studied demonology and supposedly know a lot more on the subject. We are talking about pioneer days.

...it was clear that Peter Hosein was truly touched by God supernaturally

Those things that took place, the direct spiritual intervention in his life, I do not think I can escape those. I've read books, I have been to universities; and they have had their impact on me. But the experiences I am describing here, I think they are the experiences that stand out most in my own life. And I would say that based on those that I am describing, and those alone (and there were so many more of similar nature), it was clear that Peter Hosein was truly touched by God supernaturally and was converted not as a result of any intellectual pursuit. His ministry—the success of his ministry—was not in his presentations, though he was quite an eloquent speaker. It had to be God divinely anointing him.

Then, of course, the final encounter was his death. I was asked to speak one night during the services, and I preached again at his memorial one year after. When I preached at those services I said to myself, "I will now live and preach for him and for me." Everything I do, I do in the shadow of this man. I do not seek to imitate him; I do not speak like him. In my early days I did, but now I have gone into a different direction. I am still solidly Pentecostal evangelical. I believe in all the values he taught. And even at times when I am tempted to depart from some of those early values, I cannot escape the experience of God's anointing. It is difficult sometimes for the intellectual approach to overrule.

Thank goodness for that!

This ends the testimony of Dr. Stephen Mohammed.

Chapter 11
THE WORLD IS HUNGRY FOR GOD

WE HAVE JUST read how God used an obedient servant to represent Him in the Caribbean, and how, through a ministry closely modeled after that of Christ and His early disciples, much fruit was harvested. God has not forgotten the rest of the world, and that is the reason for this epic narrative—the reason behind Peter's ministry and the reason for this book.

The roots of Peter Hosein's ministry were planted a little over 2,000 years ago; they took root at the point of entry of Yahweh, the Creator, into the everyday life of humans here on planet Earth—the birth of Jesus of Nazareth in the town of Bethlehem in Judea.

For centuries God has appointed and empowered prophets—representatives—to speak to mankind on His behalf and tell them that:

- He exists, and has total control over all Creation—His Creation;

- His primary motivation in all eternity was to fulfill the hope and desires He had instilled in mankind prior to their rejection of Him

- Their willful broken connection with Him cut them off from the very source of life itself;

- There is a solution to all of mankind's resulting misery and death;

- The entire cost of the needed reconciliation has been born by God, and mankind need only get honest and turn to Him for help.

As you have just read, Peter Hosein carried out his assignment to bring these truths to his appointed field of mission as a Holy Spirit anointed apostle ("sent one"), in a manner similar to that of St. Paul, who modeled his ministry on that of Jesus.

This carefully authenticated account of the ministry of a true twentieth century *functional* apostle—as contrasted with the original Twelve appointed by Jesus to the *office* of apostle—has been presented (1) to help to ignite faith for salvation in the heart, mind, and body of those genuinely seeking God; (2) to help expand and further empower the ministry potential and effectiveness of those already called into gospel service; and (3) to help put to rest the rather widely held error that is currently damaging the twenty-first century church: cessationism. (*Cessationism* is a destructive error—perhaps heresy—that claims, with virtually no normative scriptural basis, that all supernatural ministry in the church age was terminated by the Spirit either at the death of the original twelve apostles or at the closing of the Cannon of the Holy Scriptures, perhaps at the Council of Nicaea.) Jesus said, "My sheep hear [recognize, listen to] My voice, and I know them" (John 10:27, NKJV). May I suggest that any of us that get stuck in this issue go to Him; He is able to give the wisdom necessary to settle the question (James 1:5).

We have a job to do before His soon return. We must

reach out to the millions of spiritually hungry souls, both locally and abroad, that are waiting for our word of hope. Let's do it with all the help the Spirit of God has available for us to excel in this work. Let Him guide us, speak through us, and work wonders through us! Often when words in themselves are ineffective in grabbing the attention of many "comfortable," self-sufficient, complacent people in our neighborhoods, these same people can be jarred into acute awareness of the startling reality of the existence of the paranormal realm that completely surrounds them: "Jesus said, 'My kingdom is not of this world. If it were, my servants would fight to prevent my arrest by the Jewish leaders. But now my kingdom is from another place'" (John 18:36).

There are people all over this planet sitting in Christian churches, Muslim mosques, and Hindu temples crying out for the assurance of God's love. And God is even hungrier for their fellowship:

> For the eyes of the Lord run to and fro throughout the whole earth, to shew himself strong in the behalf of them whose heart is perfect toward him.
> —2 Chronicles 16:9a, kjv

> I urge, then, first of all, that requests, prayers, intercession and thanksgiving be made for all people— for kings and all those in authority, that we may live peaceful and quiet lives in all godliness and holiness. This is good, and pleases God our Savior, who wants *all people* to be saved and to come to a knowledge of the truth.
> —1 Timothy 2:1–4, emphasis added

He is even reaching out to them as He did in a sovereign way with Peter Hosein when there seems to be no human

agent available to carry forth His words of love and reconciliation. The real problem in the world is that people
in general have rejected God's love and gone to incred-
ible efforts to create their own form of conscience soothing
self-justification. But it doesn't really help because the guilt
is still there, and so is the incessant, subconscious fear of
God's ultimate retribution. Man lives in fear of death, and
after that the judgment that will follow. We are in a form of
"cold war" with God; there is no peace.

But God is love. And, He is still reaching out, even where
there is no human witness or when the soul He is seeking
is too hardened to hear the normally convincing words of a
Spirit-led man or woman of God.

One beautiful morning in the spring of 1996, Doug
Norwood, my ministry partner, and I were just entering
one of the historic gateways into the old city of Jerusalem.
We had the day free from the normally hectic schedule of
the tour we were on through Israel. We had not gone more
than twenty or thirty feet before one of the many Arab tour
guides approached us, looking for a paid assignment. We
thanked him, apologetically, indicating that we had pretty
much set our own agenda for the day, and that since this
was Doug's third trip, we had sufficient knowledge of the
geography and the culture to get by. However, we felt led
to ask him what he thought of all the many Christian historical sites and of the many acts of divine intervention by
God that these sites represented. In fact, we asked him what
he thought of Christ. We were blessed by his response, but
not really shocked. There have been more and more tales
coming out of the "10/40 Window" of God's direct intervention. (The 10/40 Window refers to evangelistic "target area"
of the world in the eastern hemisphere bounded by the lati-
tudinal lines of ten degrees north and forty degrees north.)

The guide looked over his shoulder in both directions, then leaned toward us in confidence and began to describe dreams that he had had of Jesus Christ. He even mentioned that he knew of others with similar experiences.

The accounts of God's divine intervention in these troubling times are not uncommon. In a paper prepared recently I listed a number of such accounts reported by Christian missionaries all over the world. Since it is illegal to preach religious conversion in many Middle Eastern and Asiatic countries today, often a capital offense, God is quite regularly filling the void through angelic visitations, dreams, and visions.

Exciting illustrations

In his book *Beyond Imagination*, Dick Eastman reported on the encouraging information contained in the August 1995 letter to Campus Crusade partners by Dr. Bill Bright. Apparently thousands of Arabs in North Africa and the Middle East responded to a radio program aired throughout the region recounting dreams experienced by them prior to the broadcast wherein Jesus appeared to them, and said, "I am the Way." When they heard the program, they were able to begin to understand the dreams and asked for more information on "this person called Jesus."

Dr. Bright also reported that many Muslims in Algeria had experienced dreams of Christ wherein many of their friends had dreams so similar that the actual words spoken to them by the Lord were identical. A woman from that same region, nearing the end of her prison term for illegal political activities, had a vision of Jesus in her cell. Jesus personally explained the plan of salvation to her; she surrendered her heart to Him and went on to become a minister to many in her area as a Campus Crusade staff worker.

Similar reports come out of the Kashmir. Jalaluddin, a devout Muslim, had studied the Qur'an for years. Although never having met a Christian worker and having no knowledge of the gospel, Jala became dissatisfied his experience of the Divine. The peace he sought could not be found. Then, one night, a Man in a white robe appeared to him in a dream; He asked, "Do you want real peace?" "Yes, I am seeking peace, but I've been unable to find it."

"Read the Holy Scripture."

"What is the Holy Scripture, and where can I get it?"

"The Holy Scripture is the Holy Bible, and you can get it from the India Every Home Crusade, [address withheld], in Lucknow."

Jalaluddin sat up in bed. He grabbed a piece of paper and wrote down the address. A few days later, a letter arrived at the EHC office, containing the following statement,

> I don't know who you people are or whether this address is correct, but I am writing exactly what I was told in a dream. If you receive this, would you please immediately send me something that is called a "Holy Bible"?

After completing four lessons, and the reading of the New Testament, Jala wrote once more to the EHC office with the following remarkable statement: "The course has enlightened me about the reality of the Trinity, as well as the truth about the Sonship of Jesus Christ." That a person of his particular religious persuasion could acknowledge these truths is proof of the transforming power of the gospel when applied by the Holy Spirit.[1]

This anecdote was of a passive nature in that God worked sovereignly without direct human initiation. The following involves God's blessing of the active work of one of his servants.

One day in a major Middle Eastern city with a population of over a million, a young convert to Christianity was handing out gospel tracts door-to-door. At one apartment the resident, a young businessman, was home. He took the tract, recognized the Christian thrust, and went into a threatening tirade, tearing up the tract. The Christian worker was shaken by the threats, but went his way, delivering more tracts.

That night the businessman was awakened by a pair of hands that grabbed his shoulders, shaking him. The man flailed around, trying to ward off the unseen being. He jumped up, switched on the light, and saw the room to be empty. He cried out, "Who are you? What do you want?" The response was, "You have torn up the truth. The message you were given by the visitor at your door was God's truth that points to eternal life. It tells of the only way to lasting peace and happiness, and you have torn it up."

The voice then gave the man the address of the worker and advised him to go to that person's house the next morning, which he did. The businessman was led to the Lord, and ultimately became a worker himself, after being ostracized from his own family and made subject to a death threat.[2] Eastman reports that these kinds of experiences are "increasing dramatically on a global scale."

In his book *The Unseen Face of Islam*, Bill Musk reports on a number of similar, recent "power encounters" involving the conversion of devout followers in Britain and Turkey to Christianity.[3] Another type of power encounter is that experienced in public displays where God reveals His superior authority over the powers of darkness. In his article, "Biblical Foundations of Praying for Muslims," Colin

Chapman reports on such an event from another time and place. In *The Life of Muhammad* by Ibn Ishaq (d. AD 767), there is an account of the coming of Christianity to an area in southwest Arabia. The people challenged a Christian ascetic from Syria that if he were successful in cursing a palm tree worshipped by the people, they would turn to Christ. He prayed, and then cursed the tree in God's name. It died; and the people became Christians.[4] As far-fetched as it may seem, this same sort of power encounters are in evidence today and their effect in adding credibility to the presentation of the gospel is still valid.

My partner experienced a similar miracle some years ago in Venezuela. The ground around a tree, sacred to the local Hindu community where he was ministering, was cursed one day in his presence. The moment words were issued forth, a cloud of birds flew from the tree in a state of panic. The next day the tree was completely dead.

In his book *Touching the Soul of Islam*, Bill Musk reports the account of a missionary who asked God's help to protect the life of a new Christian from his own family's brutal per-secution. In an apparent answer to prayer, a "shining figure" appeared during the night to the father of the young con-vert. He spoke directly to the man, concluding with, "If you touch your son again, you are going to die. He is showing you the way to salvation. Listen to him." The father became a Christian the next day.[5]

In a recent newsletter to its supporters, the *JESUS* Film Project reported yet another direct intervention of God as one of their African teams worked its way from village to village in what their team leaders called a "very tough loca-tion." The team was doing about six outreaches per week, showing the *JESUS* film, a very accurate presentation of the life of Jesus during His earthly ministry. Their next stop was a very large village, and an advance man was sent to make arrangements. When the team leader arrived, the worker was fruitlessly trying to persuade the chief. He did not want anything to do with "Jesus." His response was something like this: "I am a [not a Christian]. We have never allowed any other religion. You will do nothing here!"

Led by the Spirit, the team leader respectfully replied, "We are coming here to show you and your people the *JESUS* film, preach the gospel, and heal the sick."

"What did you say? Heal the sick? Really? Is that possible?"

"Yes, if you allow us to show the *JESUS* film and preach the gospel."

In a moment or two, following a glance toward his second in command, the chief turned back to the leader. "Really? Heal the sick? This we want to see."

The equipment was unloaded in the large soccer field. About 5,000 people saw the film. While it was being shown, the team leader went to his car to pray, seeking the Lord in deep intercession and asking Him for a word for the people. When the film was over he noticed that the people had been deeply moved. Over the microphone he asked how many people recognized a need for a Savior. Almost all hands were raised. All across the stadium they cried, "We want our sins to be forgiven." They pleaded to God for mercy. The entire crowd was led in a prayer of salvation. Then the leader told the people that Jesus wants to heal the sick. About a dozen with back problems came forward and were instantly healed. Then an eight-year-old deaf boy received his hearing. People kept coming and were healed.

Then the chief asked for, and was given, the mic. He spoke to his people. "What you have just seen is real. God is with [this man] and these people. Now bring all the sick from the village." They did, and they came. Even a young girl, totally blind from birth, was brought by her father. She saw her father that night for the first time in her life.

This sort of thing seems to be happening in greater numbers these days. I just received a forwarded copy of a missionary's report from India. Similar displays of supernatural power are being seen there on a regular basis. As the gospel penetrates more and more into the unreached areas of that huge nation, divine manifestations of God's supernatural power are being reported in increasing numbers.

Should we not all pray that the Lord would honor us, here in the more developed nations, with the favor of His manifest presence as we repent of the lukewarm quality of faith so prevalent here in our ultra-materialistic societies? We have seen the benefits of a totally surrendered life, the life embedded in Peter Hosein, a man whose primary assault weapon against the kingdom of darkness was prayer and fasting.

Chapter 12
GOD'S OFFER OF PEACE

JUST WHAT IS the secret to peace with God? What was the real heart of Peter Hosein's message of hope? Can such a question as, "Is there really life after death," be answered?

The answers are found in what is commonly known as the gospel—the good news of God's means for salvation through the death and resurrection of *Isa* (Arabic for Jesus) the Messiah (anointed one). I have summarized below this message of hope that is found in the "Book" (Qur'anic term for the Holy Bible).

SUMMARY OF THE GOSPEL

From the very dawn of creation, God's relationship with mankind has been of a miraculous nature. He created the universe out of nothing and then created the first man as the object of His affection out of that same nothing. This man, Adam, was designed to be responsive, reactive, and relational with his Lord. He was given a nature that was creative, curious, independent, self conscious, and capable of loving, honoring, and trusting God. God's love for Adam was so great and so selfless, that He was even willing to share this man's love with that of another person whom He would create in a design complementary to that of Adam— the woman, Eve.

What was God's ultimate purpose in developing this

visible universe of matter and relationships? We can only learn the full answer if and when we meet the Lord face-to-face in heaven, in bodies freed from the limitations of these flesh and blood "houses" in which we currently dwell. The desire to obtain the truth of this great mystery is so much a part of man that the fear of missing out on the conclusion is rather like what we experience when we are threatened with the possibility of missing the last act of a great play. Unfortunately, the result of missing this one is of infinitely greater and more horrifying consequences.

I really think that this is why no one wants to die without learning the answer to life, or at least being assured that the truth will eventually be made known. We are told in God's written Word that life after death for those who have been accepted by Him as His associates forever will be more satisfying and wonderful than can be comprehended by our present finite minds.

Throughout history, scholars have tried to come up with the answer to this mystery. Men and women struggle with this great puzzle all through life, many fearful that their actions have disqualified them from this greatest of all satisfactions. Mankind's first act of disqualification took place when Eve decided to rebel against God's love-motivated warning. Why she really believed that the conflicting advice of one of God's own created beings should take precedence, we have yet to learn. We do know that Satan, her instigator, had already failed in his attempt to elevate himself to a position of authority above that of God. How ludicrous for the created to try to unseat his or her creator! We have been told in the Bible that:

> The heart is deceitful above all things and beyond
> cure. Who can understand it?
>
> —JEREMIAH 17:9

All human thoughts and actions not specifically con-
ceived and executed under the guidance and control of the
Holy Spirit of God are known as *sins*, or *trespasses*. From the
very moment we are old enough to make conscious choices
in life, these breaches of relationship begin to alienate us
from Him. In fact, if we were able to look into the invisible
world of spirit beings, we would find that sins actually sepa-
rate us from His presence. It is not that He hates us; but that
being the Holy God that He is, He cannot look upon sin.
The overall state of separation created by the sinning party,
the *sinner*, is also called "sin." (Perhaps we should refer to
this state of alienation as "sin.")

In any case, I cannot explain the mystery of sin, but God
knew it would come into being and had already prepared
the means of reconciliation—the plan to repair the damage
done by man's rebellion. He even provided the way for
us to be restored to the peaceful, eternity-bound track to
which so many of us are drawn. Unfortunately, the road is
narrow and those that will actually arrive are few; the road
to destruction is broad, and the masses seem to be flocking
there. Jesus (Isa) the Messiah said,

> Enter through the narrow gate. For wide is the gate
> and broad is the road that leads to destruction, and
> many enter through it. But small is the gate and
> narrow the road that leads to life, and only a few
> find it.
>
> MATTHEW 7:13–14

Choosing the Way of Truth

I am glad that the Lord has seen fit to restore me and that I am one of those that have chosen the way of truth (see John 14:6). It was certainly not by my own effort, however; and if God Himself had not prepared a way back, I would certainly have been among the "lost." (Incidentally, I invite you, dear reader, to join me in this wonderful journey if you have not already done so. I will elaborate on the details a bit later.)

It was this hunger for eternity, and the need for the assurance of his acceptance onto the "paths of righteousness" (Ps. 23:3, KJV) required for winning the race of life that drew young Hakim Hosein into the very words of life found in the Book laying on the shelf in his brother's shop.

In my own search, I was hindered by my affinity for scientific proof of matters that can only be understood through the eyes of faith. My earlier training and practice in the profession of engineering did not really prepare me for the realm of the spirit. Nevertheless, this supernatural God of the universe condescended to temporarily set aside His own laws of nature and visibly and audibly reveal Himself to me mid morning one Saturday in October 1972.

My experience was similar to that of another man of God whose life is depicted in the Word of God. The man, originally known as Saul of Tarsus, a Roman citizen of Jewish birth, so hungered for the truth of God that he spent his early years studying at the feet of some of the greatest religious scholars of his time. Unfortunately, Saul's analytical mind was as crippling to him as mine was to me. Furthermore, he used human logic in planning his attack on those that understood God in a different way from what he did. It took the divine intervention of God to break him loose from his "religious bondage" much the way I was freed from my bondage to the secular, scientific worldview.

If you will look into chapter 9 of the Book of Acts in the Holy Bible, and further read an expansion of that account found in chapter 1 of the Book of Galatians, you will learn that God literally knocked Saul to the ground as he was in the middle of a trip from Jerusalem to Damascus. Saul was on a mission to persecute the "people of the Way" (later referred to in Antioch as "Christians") who were living in Damascus, the capital of Syria. The Lord spoke to Saul, identified Himself as Jesus, the Messiah, asked why he was persecuting Him, and then temporarily blinded him, giving him some time for serious thought! God's purpose for the encounter was to get Saul's attention and then reveal to him His plan for the reconciliation of man to Himself and His path to eternal life. The really interesting thing is that Saul, who Jesus then renamed Paul, was sent *directly into the heart of Arabia where Jesus personally revealed to him His message of salvation*—the message known in Christianity as the gospel, *the message referred to in Islam as the Injil.* There was no chance of Paul misunderstanding this extremely crucial message. Remember, he received it directly by revelation from the Messiah. The scriptures state the following:

> For you have heard of my previous way of life in Judaism, how intensely I persecuted the church of God and tried to destroy it. I was advancing in Judaism beyond many Jews of my own age and was extremely zealous for the traditions of my fathers. But when God, who set me apart from birth and called me by his grace, was pleased to reveal his Son in me so that I might preach him among the Gentiles, I did not consult any man, nor did I go up to Jerusalem

to see those who were apostles before I was, but I went immediately into Arabia and later returned to Damascus.

—GALATIANS 1:13–17

Was Paul really qualified to convey this crucial message to the entire Gentile world? Immediately following his initial encounter with Jesus, the blinded Paul was led by hand to Damascus and to the home of a believer. While Paul was praying and fasting there, another believer, a disciple of Jesus, was approached by the Lord. The following passage found in the Bible describes what took place and includes Jesus' direct authorization to Paul to proclaim the gospel on His behalf.

> The Lord told him, "Go to the house of Judas on Straight Street and ask for a man from Tarsus named Saul, for he is praying. In a vision he has seen a man named Ananias come and place his hands on him to restore his sight." "Lord," Ananias answered, "I have heard many reports about this man and all the harm he has done to your saints in Jerusalem. And he has come here with authority from the chief priests to arrest all who call on your name." But the Lord said to Ananias, "Go! This man is my chosen instrument to carry my name before the Gentiles and their kings and before the people of Israel. I will show him how much he must suffer for my name."
>
> —ACTS 9:11–16

This authority is also given to Muslims in their Holy book, the Qur'an as follows:

> If thou wert in doubt / As to what We have revealed / Unto thee, then ask those Who have been reading /

The Book from before thee: / The Truth (Haqq) hath indeed come To thee from thy Lord: / So be in nowise / Of those in doubt.

—SURAH 10:94[1]

Also:

We have sent thee / Inspiration, as We sent it / To Noah and the Messengers After him: We sent / Inspiration to Abraham, Isma'il, Isaac, Jacob / And the Tribes, to Jesus, Job, Jonah, Aaron, and Solomon, / And to David We gave The Psalms. Of some messengers We have / Already told thee the story; / Of others we have not—And to Moses Allah spoke direct—Messengers who gave good news / As well as warning, / That mankind, after (the coming) Of the messengers, should have / No plea against Allah: / For Allah is Exalted in Power, Wise.

—SURAH 4:163–165[2]

It is worth noting that about 600 years before Muhammad received his revelation from an angel *in Arabia*, Saint Paul received the true gospel as a direct revelation from Jesus Christ during his stay *in Arabia*.

Just what is this gospel (*Injil*) that Paul was so excited about? Well, he more or less describes it as follows:

- All men have sinned and fall short of God's glory, thus forfeiting eternal life, and are consigned to a life of disobedience, guilt, and the fear of ultimate retribution. (See Romans 3:23.)

- But, the gift of God is eternal life through the substitutionary death of Jesus on the cross.

He suffered our punishment for us. Why?
Who can explain God's infinite mercy? (See
Romans 6:23.)

- If a person will confess with his or her mouth,
  'Jesus is Lord,' and is able to believe in their
  heart that Jesus died for all of our sins and
  then rose again to life—proving His power
  over life and death—that person will be saved.
  (See Romans 10:9–10.)

Dear reader: If, at this point, you realize (a) that you are
an unrighteous person—a sinner—and fall short of God's
standard for acceptance into His eternal kingdom, (b) that
you have never experienced His forgiveness and the joy
of having all guilt eradicated, and (c) that you have never
invited Him to come into your life as Master, may I suggest
that you offer the following verbal plea to Him with a sin-
cere heart without any qualification or reservation:

Dear Lord Jesus: I acknowledge my sins and ask that
You forgive me and heal me of my sin nature. I invite
You to come and live Your life in me as both my Lord
and my Savior. I ask, also, that You would baptize
me with Your Holy Spirit to enable me for righteous
living and Holy service. Thank You. Amen.

My own encounter with God was quite remarkable. I
know that many people are skeptical of the possibility of

the Creator of the universe taking time out of His busy schedule to visit a simple human being such as myself. However, it is only because of our limiting of God's awesome capabilities that such a thought can enter our minds. The Bible is quite clear in such statements as:

> And without faith it is impossible to please God, because anyone who comes to him must believe that he exists and that *he rewards those who earnestly seek him.*
> —HEBREWS 11:6, EMPHASIS ADDED

> All things have been committed to me by my Father. No one knows who the Son is except the Father, and no one knows who the Father is except the Son *and those to whom the Son chooses to reveal him.*
> —LUKE 10:22, EMPHASIS ADDED

Although I was a regular churchgoer, I was not absolutely sure that God really existed. Furthermore, should this doubt be confirmed, there was, then, no life after death and no hope of a future existence. Life would be without meaning. I was not happy about my state of unbelief; and when I expressed it to my spiritual advisors, they could give me no satisfaction. I read books, listened to religious broadcasts, all to no avail. I was dissatisfied with who I was and with the apparent state of hypocrisy in which I existed.

First, I knew that my life was not holy according to the standards I had been taught in church. But how could that be changed? Secondly, I had my spiritual doubts, and that alone seemed to be sinful. Thirdly, I was convinced from my own observations that there was a breed of people in society who seemed to be able to be good and righteous, almost without effort. I was not one of these; so, my case was really hopeless.

Then, one day while reading a book about God's miraculous intervention into the lives of a group of young people— people seemingly without hope (such as me), it dawned on me that I might have been wrong in my approach to Him. I suddenly got very truthful and admitted my weaknesses and defects to the Lord I made a transaction with Him in which I agreed to surrender control of my entire life, assuming, of course, that He exists. I didn't test Him. I simply acknowledged my inability to believe and to obey. He met me right there. I had an awesome experience. I was literally washed clean of my sins; I was given a brief experience of heaven where I saw and experienced things beyond description; my eyes were healed of a defect; I was shown who Jesus really was; and, finally, I was given this direct charge by Him: "You must tell everyone that you can, for the rest of your life, that I exist!"

It was during one of my efforts to respond obediently to His call on my life that I was led to meet Peter. As you have just read, this remarkably real God does remarkably real things in this very real universe; and He isn't finished yet!

NOTES

INTRODUCTION
1. George Grant, *The Last Crusader: The Untold Story of Christopher Columbus* (Wheaton, IL: Crossway Books, 1992), 109.
2. Ibid., 121.

CHAPTER 2
YOUNG PRIEST IN TRAINING
1. Abdullah Yusuf Ali, *The Meaning of the Holy Qur'an*, (Beltsville, MD: Amana Publications, 1989).

CHAPTER 3
PETER'S FIRST MISSIONARY JOURNEY
1. Gordon Lindsay (1909–1973) was the founder of Christ for the Nations. One of CFN's ministries, even today, is the provision of financial assistance to young churches in the mission field. (See https://cfn.org/church-roofs.)

CHAPTER 4
THE MIRACLE OF SAINT VINCENT
1. *Cessationism* is a theological position that believes that the supernatural ministry of the first century apostles appointed by the Lord Jesus ended either at their death or at the closing of the canon of scripture in the third century AD.

CHAPTER 6
SPIRITUAL WARFARE
1. *Savior*: a redeemer, one who pays off the debt of a kinsman who cannot afford to pay his own debt. In this case the debt was eternal damnation in hell. Jesus died on the cross of Calvary in Jerusalem to atone for the sins of all who turn to Him in repentance and receive Him as their Lord. The Book of Hebrews affirms the kinship of those who accept Christ. It tells us that Christ is pleased to call us brothers (and sisters).

CHAPTER 9
REFLECTIONS OF A "PK"

1.   The institution of indentured servanthood, which has its roots in Bible times, permitted families to leave their lives of poverty and travel to new horizons of opportunity by offering themselves as collateral for the huge sum of money advanced to them for their trip.

CHAPTER 11
THE WORLD IS HUNGRY FOR GOD

1.   Dick Eastman, *Beyond Imagination: A Simple Plan to Save the World* (Grand Rapids, MI: Chosen Books, 1997), 200–201.

2.   Ibid., 192–194.

3.   Bill Musk, *The Unseen Face of Islam* (Crowborough, UK: Monarch Publications, 1989), 239–255.

4.   Colin Chapman, "Biblical Foundations of Praying for Muslims," in *Muslims and Christians on the Emmaus Road* (Monrovia, CA: MARC Publications, 1989), 317.

5.   Bill A. Musk, *Touching the Soul of Islam* (Crowborough, UK: MARC, 1995), 87.

CHAPTER 12
GOD'S OFFER OF PEACE

1.   Abdullah Yusuf Ali.

2.   Ibid.

ABOUT THE AUTHOR

THE AUTHOR, WHO holds a B.S. in Civil Engineering and an M.A. in Christian Ministry, is a former executive with an international architectural/engineering/construction firm, a former military officer, and has ministered in international church revitalization work and prison ministry. He is currently pastoring an Assemblies of God church in the U.S.